Fruits of the
Tree
of Life

New Discoveries

Fruits of the
Tree
of Life

New Discoveries

Peter Benes

New England Historic
Genealogical Society

AmericanAncestors.org

2023

ISBN-13: 978-0-88082-415-6
Library of Congress Control Number: 2022945317

Front cover image: "Gloucester April 30.th 1795—Family Record—Drawn by William Saville" for the 1762 marriage of Capt. John Woodbury and Susanna Lane. Watercolor and pen on paper. Gloucester, Massachusetts, 1795. Collection of the Cape Ann Museum.

End paper images: (front) by J. Russell. *Map of the northern, or, New England states of America*, 1795. (back) by Tobias Conrad Lotter. *A map of the most inhabited part of New England*, 1776. Maps courtesy of the Norman B. Leventhal Map & Education Center at the Boston Public Library.

NEW ENGLAND HISTORIC GENEALOGICAL SOCIETY
AmericanAncestors.org
Boston, Massachusetts
2023

Table of Contents

Acknowledgments

This book is dedicated to the memory of Gregory H. Laing (1947–2007), Special Collections Librarian at the Haverhill Public Library. The author acknowledges the kind help of Victoria Taylor Hawkins, formerly Curator of Collections at the Nantucket Historical Association, who provided transparencies of their collection in the 1980s, and Michael R. Harrison, present Obed Macy Director of Research and Collections at that institution, and Ralph Marie Henke, Photograph Archive Specialist there. The author also acknowledges the long-standing help of Judith N. Lund, who provided the New Bedford busk and located several family registers for this study. Also contributing were Arthur B. and Sybil B. Kern of Pawtucket, R.I.; in addition, Stacey A. Fraser, Collections and Outreach Manager at the Lexington Historical Society, and Nancy Carlisle, Curator at Historic New England, kindly read portions of the manuscript; and Marshall W. S. Swan, former president of Sandy Bay Historical Society. Other assistance came from Donald R. Randall, who offered material on Joseph Odiorne; the collectors and authors Glee Krueger, Betty Ring, and Sheila Rideout, Pam Boynton, Selina Little, Stephen and Carol Huber, Amy Finkel; as well as Claudia Perry, Mary Grace Carpenter, and especially Brian S. Ehrlich, who furnished information on John Brown Copp. Donald R. Friary generously provided Maine research and arranged the photography with the Peabody Essex Museum. Jane Montague Benes, Mina Benes-Rosecan, and Tuska Benes contributed significantly to the genealogical research and to the search for additional artifacts.

The author also wishes to thank Barbara Mathews and Martha McNamara for organizing the conference "Art of Remembrance: Family Art and Memory in New England," where an initial version of this study was given under the title "'Art Thou a Son? Or a Daugter?': Compelling New Evidence on Decorated Family Trees in New England, 1770–1850," held at the Deerfield-Wellesley Symposium, Deerfield, Massachusetts, 18 March 2017, and sponsored by Historic Deerfield, Inc., and the Grace Slack McNeil Program for Studies in American Art at Wellesley College. At the New England Historic Genealogical Society, the author is grateful for the enduring support of D. Brenton Simons, President and CEO, who also greatly assisted this effort in the years 2000 through 2002 with the publication of *The Art of Family: Genealogical Artifacts in New England*; Timothy Salls, former Manager of Manuscript Collections, who kindly supplied images of items in their collection; Sharon Inglis, Publishing Director; Cécile Engeln, Assistant Publishing Director; and Ellen Maxwell, Publications Design Manager, all working during the trying times of the pandemic, as well as freelance copyeditor Anna Williams. Finally, the author wishes to express sincere thanks to the institutional and individual owners of family register documents, embroideries, and other artifacts cited in the study for their willingness to allow them to be published.

Peter Benes
10 March 2021

Abbreviations Used in This Book

Ancestry.com = [database online] Provo or Lehi, Utah: Ancestry.com Operations, Inc.
HNE = Historic New England
LHS = Lexington Historical Society
NEHGS = New England Historic Genealogical Society | American Ancestors
NHA = Nantucket Historical Association
SBHS = Sandy Bay Historical Society, Rockport, Massachusetts
SPNEA = Society for the Preservation of New England Antiquities
VR = Vital Records

Please note: All figures within square brackets […] are checklist items appearing in **Appendix: Checklist of Twin-Heart and Multi-heart Family Registers.**

List of Figures

Introduction

The formative years of 1785 to 1825 were pivotal in the building of federal America. The country was obliged to disentangle itself from British political affairs; to survey its new northern border with Canada; to write and adjust a new unifying constitution; and to produce and train a new naval force. On a more personal level, it was also a time for Americans of European descent to spell and pronounce words uniformly[1] and to recognize their familial relationships, which had been gradually developing in a colonial and post-colonial setting. While few calligraphic and genealogical artists emerged as national painters, some found ways to memorialize and celebrate these ties for current and future generations and began to advertise their talents. Henry Williams, a successful Boston miniature, portrait, and profile painter, announced in 1806 he would make "Drawings of Family Records, neatly fil[l]ed up."[2] Unfortunately, no example of Williams's calligraphic or genealogical work is now known. Nevertheless, decorated and embroidered registers were starting to appear in everyday household probate inventories. The appraisers of the estate of Obed Marshall of Nantucket in 1817 began a list of his personal possessions with a "Family Record c[en]ts .50"—a watercolor that has survived to this day *(Figures 1 and 2)* [checklist 6].[3] This document, using intertwining rose stems issuing from a pair of touching hearts, celebrates the 1767 marriage of Marshall (1744–1817) and Susanna Burnell (1747–1814) and the birth of their seven children between 1767 and 1787, and it records the death of one child, Thomas, in 1768. The artist was Edward D. Burke, an Irish schoolteacher then living on Nantucket, who carefully printed each spouse's name at the base of the crossing vines and each child's name on the attached flowering rose blossoms—one of three similar family registers known to be made by Burke while staying on the island. Just as Henry Williams promised, Burke "fil[l]ed" his record with the genealogy of the Marshall family, keeping them in artistic touch with the larger ancestral memory of southeastern Massachusetts.

We will probably never know if Burke came up with the twin-heart motif as part of his private repertoire or whether he simply followed the expectations of Obed Marshall's family or those of the island community as a whole. What we do know is that Burke helped put a finishing touch on the widespread practice of using

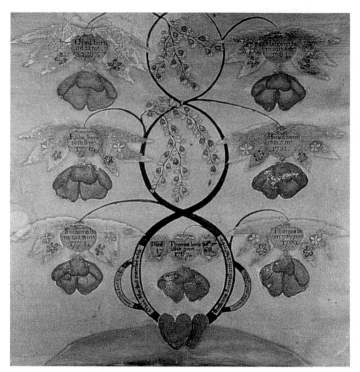

Figure 1 [checklist 6]. Obed Marshall / Susanna Burnell family tree. Signed: "Edwd D. Burke, Pin[xit]." Watercolor. Nantucket, Massachusetts, circa 1794–1796. Photograph courtesy of Paul Madden.

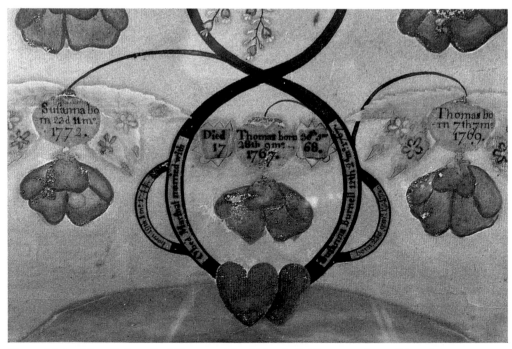

Figure 2 [checklist 6]. Detail of *Figure 1*. Obed Marshall / Susanna Burnell family tree. Photograph courtesy of Paul Madden.

Fruits of the Tree of Life

everyday emblems to create family trees that graphically documented the marriages, remarriages, births, and deaths (often cited as "lost at sea") taking place in individual Nantucket households.

Comparable documents and commemorations of people's lives were occurring elsewhere. When Rev. William Bentley visited Marblehead in 1809, his friend Ashley Bowen told him he had just given to "one of the name [Bowen]," who operated a Boston museum, "the tree of the Bowen family drawn by my pupil" [meaning Bentley's pupil, identified earlier in the diary as "HC" or Hannah Crowninshield][4]—no doubt a school-based calligraphic and genealogical exercise taught by Bentley from the days when the Salem minister offered a writing class in that town.

Fortunately, Ashley Bowen appears to have made a copy of Hannah Crowninshield's "tree" (*Figure 3*) before passing the original to the Boston museum. The copy was eventually given by Bowen's heirs to the Essex Institute and is now housed together with his diary in the library of the Peabody Essex Museum. The image consists of two vines planted firmly in the foreground holding small orbs with representations of sons and daughters spread over generations. On the left is Obadiah Bowen who arrived in America from Swansea, Wales, in 1640. On the right is Benjamin Hallowell who arrived in Boston later. After Ashley's grandfather

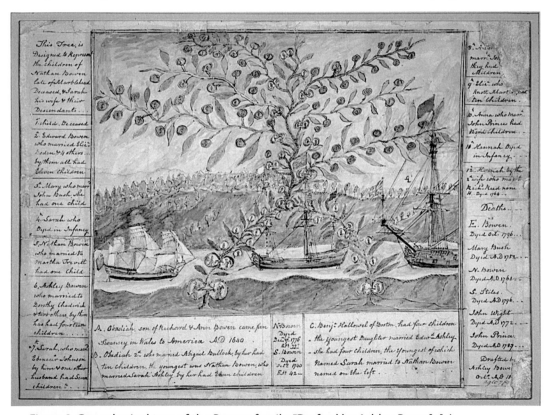

Figure 3. Genealogical tree of the Bowen family. "Drafted by Ashley Bowe[n] / Oct.ʳ A.D 18 [ ] (1804?)." Based on genealogical information provided by Hannah Crowninshield of Salem, Massachusetts. Watercolor. Courtesy of Peabody Essex Museum.

Obadiah married Abigail Bullock and produced ten children, the vines become joined with the Hallowell vine when Nathan Bowen marries Sarah Ashley, thus creating four generations of Ashley Bowen's ancestry. The scheme depicts thirteen marriages (shown by touching miniatures) and produces about sixty-five children following a schematic pattern provided by Hannah Crowninshield. We do not know if this arrangement was Hannah's or Ashley's. The image was "drafted" by Ashley Bowen and holds his signature under the date October 18[04]. It seems done in Bowen's characteristic watercolor style and reflects intimate knowledge of ships; but the genealogy was cited by Bentley as being Hannah Crowninshield's research.

Either way, like Burke's climbing rose, the crossed or intersecting vines of Bowen's genealogy and the use of flowers, fruits, or miniatures to illustrate births, as well as the rooting of initial families in mounds of earth, seem to have been part of a shared visual dialect that moved across space and time and apparently had its ultimate origin among the genealogies and histories created by medieval and early Renaissance English, French, Portuguese, and German miniaturists and calligraphers. These fourteenth- and fifteenth-century scribes highlighted progeny by means of trees or vines or even bloodlines reaching from the heart or torso of a prone ancestor to his or her descendants. In the illustration shown in *Figure 4,* for example, taken from a circa-1370 German manuscript tracing the genealogical origin of the Christ Child, the scribe illuminates Mary's birth to Joachym and Anna by a beautiful flowering stalk issuing from a tree of life spread out below them. In New England, traces of this naive tradition still persisted four hundred years later when tree- and vine-themed family registers—many issuing from joined hearts—were typically framed and hung on a wall or protected in a box or desk where they served as decorative reminders for families to honor their forebears. Other visual metaphors serving New Englanders' genealogies included linked or touching chains; interconnected circles; squares joined by vines or tendrils; floral or architectural signboards; and a variety of contiguous, superimposed, or linked heart emblems.[5] It was a language as distinct and regionally specific as those that governed eighteenth-century and early nineteenth-century American speech, including local pronunciation patterns, and even such items as tavern signs, maritime flags, and military banners.[6]

While rarely encountered today, Edward D. Burke's twin-heart motif was certainly one of the most arresting of the local genealogical variations found in eastern and coastal New England during that period, and it characterized almost all known decorated family registers produced on Nantucket Island and Martha's Vineyard. (See Appendix, checklist items 1–22.) In these documents, the parents are represented by overlapping or contiguous hearts located at the bottom; the births of children, by flowers attached to stems of vines issuing from the paired matrimonial hearts; second or third marriages, by a new set of hearts and a new set of stems; the deaths of children or their parents, by faded, shriveled, or broken flowers and stems; and the deaths of

Figure 4. Joachym and Anna giving birth to Mary. Below a tree of life is rising from a prone ancestor. Circa 1370. Page 8 in *Speculum Humanae Salvationis,* "Tree of Jessie." Westfalen od. Koln.um. Courtesy of Technische Universität Darmstadt, tudigit.ulb.tu-darmstadt.de/show/Hs-2505.

parents, by cut-off vines and small banners. At least we have assumed they meant these things to Nantucketers of the late eighteenth and early nineteenth centuries. In a sense, the act of reading and deciphering these documents is like eavesdropping on a conversation among family members that took place two centuries ago. What we see constitutes a small fraction of genealogical conceptualizing and symbolism that was shared by Nantucket family members and probably by their immediate neighbors. Unfortunately, we are unable to interrupt their discourse to question why they seldom discussed these memorial objects in their letters or mentioned them in their diaries. Instead we are left to enumerate them, to try to learn their date and maker, and to ascertain the origins of their designs.

This author's recent discovery of fifty-one additional decorated registers that used Burke's twin-heart motif (or one of its several New England variants) provides an opportunity for a closer look at how graphic artwork and embroideries produced by calligraphers, amateur artists, and needlework teachers and students celebrated family genealogy during this formative period. Many of these "new" pieces were located through online searching of archives: documentary evidence from public auctions; price-checking references; items submitted with widows' petitions for government pensions; and images posted on the internet as general genealogical information.[7] The goal here is to recast the larger conceptual, didactic, commemorative, and legal roles that these illustrated documents and embroideries played in early New England communities, as well as to reframe their geographical dispersal and intergenerational reuse. The best approach to understanding these issues is one coordinated with a close examination of local histories and genealogies. This protocol has been assiduously followed here. But the analysis of contemporary language is also helpful especially when provided by diaries. Most connections between eighteenth- and early nineteenth-century period language practices and symbols appearing on family registers are now irretrievable. But in a few instances, ties emerge. For example, an epitaph in the old Newbury, Massachusetts, burying ground for the gravestone of Henry Sewall (1615–1700) notes that "his fruitful vine, being thus disjoined, fell to the ground January the 13 following, aetat 74"—a common reference to depicting death as a broken stem, such as was used by family record artists in Nantucket. Elsewhere, Rev. Edward Taylor repeats the same tree allusion as he cautions the children mourning the death of their father in Farmington, Connecticut:

> And as for you his Buds, and Blossoms blown,
> Stems of his Root, his very Flesh and Bone,
> You needs must have great droopings, now the Tree
> Is fallen down the boughs whereof you bee.[8]

Other echoes of genealogical motifs found their way into hymns and songs. William Saville (1770–1853)—the Gloucester, Massachusetts, schoolteacher responsible for a number of signed watercolor family registers (all with twin-heart emblems)—made a "Family Record" (*Figures 5 and 6*) [checklist 29] on 30 April 1795 celebrating the marriage of Capt. John Woodbury and Susanna Lane, parents of twelve children born between 1762 and 1787. The piece, which commemorated Woodbury's death in 1790, cited Isaac Watts's familiar lamentation published in 1706:

> Farewell dear Friend a short Farewell
> Till we shall meet again above;
> In the sweet Groves where pleasures dwell
> And Trees of Life bear fruits of Love.

Saville also received commissions to draw small-scale memorials (often designed as "tombs") of deceased children and parents. In a memento mori (*Figure 7*), made for Betsy Dennison Rowe, daughter of William and Betsy Rowe of Gloucester, he again quotes Watts's poetic stanza to lament Betsy's death in 1793:

> Farewell dear Child a short farewell
> Till we shall meet again above;
> In the sweet Groves where pleasures dwell
> And Trees of Life bear fruits of Love.[9]

It is the final line of Isaac Watts's stanza, "And Trees of Life bear fruits of Love," that is the subject of this study—a cultural and linguistic analysis of a regional genealogical emblem.

Besides indicating that genealogical heart-themed watercolors and embroideries were much more common than previously supposed, the newly acquired body of evidence summarized here reveals unusual variations in the basic multiple-heart motif, which now can be broken down into several subtypes. One artist in Chelsea, Massachusetts—Edward Pratt—constructed genealogical images using a standing pear tree rising from joined hearts. A second artist provides an indication that the entwined vine emblem—a device seemingly confined to Nantucket Island and Martha's Vineyard—may actually have been thriving in other places in New England. We learn that a third artist with an apparent Boston connection—who initialed his or her work "J. P."—was active along estuary towns in New Hampshire and Maine; still another was working in Townsend, Fitchburg, and Ashby, Massachusetts. The total number of known family registers using twin-heart or multi-heart images now stands at one hundred fourteen, an increase that virtually doubles the figure compiled by this author in two earlier checklists published in 1985 and 2002.[10] Of these, approximately one-third were school taught; one-third were commissioned pieces; and one-third appear to be by amateurs. The number of known school-taught embroideries of this type produced in the presumed academy or academies for young women in Middlesex County towns now has almost doubled.

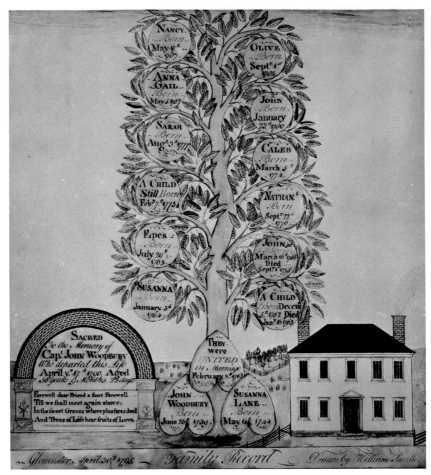

Figure 5 [checklist 29]. "Gloucester April 30.th 1795—Family Record—Drawn by William Saville" for the 1762 marriage of Capt. John Woodbury and Susanna Lane. Watercolor and pen on paper. Gloucester, Massachusetts, 1795. Collection of the Cape Ann Museum.

Figure 6 [checklist 29]. Detail of lower right of *Figure 5*. "Gloucester April 30.th 1795—Family Record—Drawn by William Saville."

Fruits of the Tree of Life

Figure 7. Memento mori for Betsy Dennison, daughter of William and Betsy Rowe of Gloucester, Massachusetts. "Drawn by William Saville 1793." Watercolor. Sandy Bay Historical Society, 281.

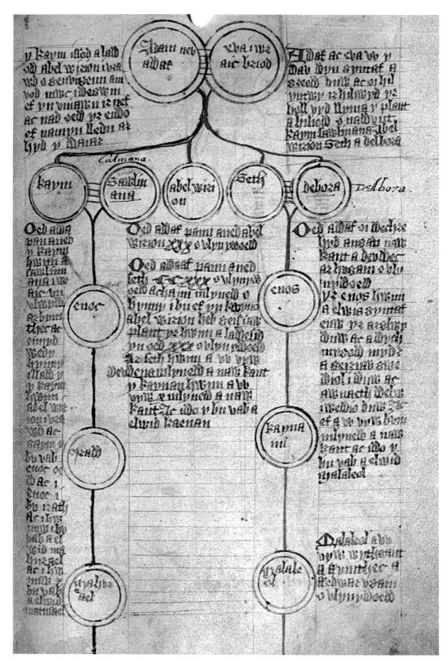

Figure 8. Detail. Genealogy and history from Adam and Eve to Asclobitotus.
Unfinished, created between 1488 and 1498. National Library of Wales, File P 63.

The Eurasian and English Origins
of the Motif Components

While it is always tempting to suggest that hearts-and-vine and hearts-and-tree motifs were an eighteenth-century decorative tradition imported from European aristocratic or merchants' circles into the newly formed social groupings in the United States, the reality is much more complex and uncertain. To fully understand the range of this visual language, we have to begin with the European and Asian backgrounds of the individual symbols. The genealogical "family tree" concept, for example, goes back to some of the earliest civilizations of the Middle East. In the Bible, the third verse of Psalm 1, the "blessed man" is likened to a "tree"

> planted by water-rivers:
> that in his season yields his fruit,
> and his leafe never withers.[11]

In the Near East, people of the pre-Christian Hebraic region, Egypt, and Persia, and later in the Ottoman Empire, made this "tree" a central concept of their genealogical perspective and world view. Later the ruling gentry shared this mindset with their subjects throughout Catholic and Protestant Europe, who in turn handed it down to families in early modern Europe—England, France, Germany, Norway, Italy, Spain, Portugal, and Holland. Ambitious European powers presumably disseminated these ideas to their American colonies either through schooling or through their retention in the memories of immigrating families.

We can trace this evolution through surviving examples. To begin with, calligraphers created genealogical designs by linking heredity through the fruiting of branches, flowers, vines, or tendrils, all growing from a common source. One early medieval-period manuscript housed at the National Library of Wales (*Figure 8*) displays Adam and Eve as two contiguous circles united by marriage ties and followed by four generations of children strung together below them with blue or red tendrils, each child listed by name (Cain and Abel among them).[12] Another example dating to the early fourteenth century (*Figure 9*) is more complex and shows Henry III listening to the bells at Westminster Abbey, with his descendants listed below. Marriages and offspring are strung together as intersecting circles, beginning with Edward I and continuing with Edmund, Margaret, Beatrice, and Katherine. A genealogy dated from 1460 to 1470—this one with the ancestors shown at the bottom—is much more historically explicit (*Figure 10*) and depicts a succession of royal descendants

Figure 9. Henry III with façade of Westminster Abbey. Miniature of Henry III with descendants linked together with intersecting circles shown below him. Manuscript dated circa 1307–1327. © The British Library, Royal MS 20 A II, f. 9r.

Fruits of the Tree of Life

Figure 10. "Typological life and genealogy of Edward IV." Miniature in colors. Parchment roll dated between 1460 and circa 1470. © The British Library, Harley 7353.

Figure 11. Detail of center of *Figure 10.* "Typological life and genealogy of Edward IV" showing Henry IV severing the stalk of his competitor. Each figure bears a first-person description about his or her role in the succession.

rising from the prone bodies (in full armor) of Henry III and Edward IV.[13] A detail of the center of the image (*Figure 11*) shows Henry IV lopping off the stalk of his competitor Richard II en route to his accession as king. The resulting typological life resembles a complex herbarium where flowered stalks reveal only the upper bodies of Englishmen and their spouses—the "flowering" half-effigies—fighting for the throne and eventually leading to the coronation of the new monarch. In each case, the stalks or vines on which these "flowering" effigies find their rank rise from the upper body of a large prone figure, presumably their lineal ancestor lying on the ground, with the stem or bloodline planted in his heart.[14]

Sometimes these "flowering" half-effigies were supplemented by linked roundels—small circles bearing the stylized miniatures of siblings, wives, and children—usually joined to their spouses or parents or offspring by ribbons or tendrils. An early example of this style is a sixteenth-century thirty-four-page genealogical chronicle of Edward VI (*Figure 12*) at the British Library. Addressing

Fruits of the Tree of Life

the birth of Adam and Eve, the final pages of this document are devoted to English royalty where rows of siblings and cousins are connected by specially colored bands. Those with the closest royal affinity are indicated with a crown, marking the succession of Edward IV, Henry VII, and Richard III, all competing for power. They, too, are tied together with each family producing multiple progeny trailing a maze of births behind them.[15] In Scotland in 1603, one painter composed a "[g]enealogical chart tracing the Tudor roots of Mary Stuart, Queen of Scots & her son James VI of Scotland & I of England," depicting fourteen framed miniature portraits beginning with Henry VII and Elizabeth and rising up through the accession of James I in 1603. Blossoming roses designate the lines of succession; the frames (not the portraits), dressed in attire that matches individual portraits, hold hands with their respective marriage partners to declare their lineage.[16]

The genealogical messages in these documents were also applied to the lives of English authors and to rules governing the attainment of polite manners. "The Progenie of Geffrey Chaucer" (*Figure 13*)—a late sixteenth-century engraving—finds the great English poet surrounded by his siblings and descendants pictured in roundels accompanied by the coats of arms of four generations of their offspring.[17] Elsewhere, in a seventeenth-century treatise on manners, the term "Gentility" (*Figure 14*) portrays what may be a married pregnant woman holding a blank hatchment looking at her ancestry on a record mounted on a fire screen standing before her. The image shows three pedigreed armorials growing in garden pots side by side; hanging above them are linkages to thirty-one progeny, each one articulated by a roundel attached to a particular plant.[18]

Nor were these types of linking and typological images limited to English-speaking people. A 1505 French manuscript of the early Renaissance (*Figure 15*) displays a complex arrangement of vines growing from the heart of the Duke of Lorraine's prone body and nourishing twenty-seven "flowering" effigies, each one nurtured by a vine leading to another farther up the chain.[19] As in their English counterpart, most of these figures are shown from the waist up; scepters define those eligible for the throne. A late fifteenth-century German genealogy of the Holy Roman Emperor by Hartmann Schedel (*Figure 16*) displays the same pattern, but this time the linking vines run between women much like an umbilical cord, going from the upper abdomen of one to the next in the succession.[20] In the early eighteenth century the genealogy compiled by Johann Michael Wilhelm von Prey zu Strasskirchen of the Bavarian aristocracy (*Figure 17*)[21] was illustrated by placing ten generations rising from a prone armor-clad figure who not only carried the weight of his progeny but three similar prone figures in the uppermost part. Another German artist created the 1773 "Stammbaum der Familie Bach" ("Family Tree of the Bach Kindred") (*Figure 18*), a document showing an ascending web of seventy-seven connected and named upside-down hearts;[22] an anonymous Spanish/Mexican artist illustrated in 1755 the five generations of the family of Antonio Joseph Cordero and the associated families of Manaldo, Gomez, Bustamante, Odante, and Ponce (*Figure 19*) using roundels instead of hearts to name the children.[23]

Quite separate from this elite or educated tradition were more popular images of marriage and love—symbols so commonly used they might even be considered as allegorical graffiti. The heart symbol, for example, was a non-biblical and non-aristocratic image that represented conjugal or familial love. This symbol was already prevalent in England and France in the fifteenth and sixteenth centuries and its representation provided decoration for many precious metal forms such as amulets, lockets, and posy rings (*Figures 20a and 20b*). The British historian Joan Evans's 1931 study, *English Posies and Posy Rings,* compiled a list of three thousand inscriptions found on them, many illustrated by twin hearts or a heart clasped by a pair of hands. Some items repeated stock phrases such as "pence de moy" (*Figure 21*); others were inscribed with an initial or a name. One heart-shaped English amulet at the Victoria and Albert Museum (*Figure 22*)— made for holding remnants of a caul—specifically cites that John Monson was born on 10 September 1597 at "12 of the clok at night." Most hearts were shown in an upright position, and pairs were usually arranged interlocking with (or touching) each other (*Figure 23*). Some hearts were illustrated inside a second one, or as part of a coterie of hearts within a heart. Other depictions show two upside-down hearts or two placed horizontally with the ends touching or overlapping.

This covert visual protocol was presumably passed along when English families crossed the Atlantic to settle in the New World in the seventeenth century. While today associated with carved tree trunks blazoned with initials and Cupid's arrow (where they serve as a symbol of mutual love, engagement, or marriage), hearts can be traced in America to eighteenth- and early nineteenth-century jewelry. The American equivalent of John Monson's caul locket is a silver heart-shaped one made for Samuel R. C. Moffat of Portsmouth, New Hampshire, about 1776.[24] In the later nineteenth century single or paired hearts also appeared on charms, pendants, jewelry boxes, rebuses, and paper valentines.[25] These symbols are particularly evident on scrimshaw objects made during periods of separation while the man served in the military or as a seaman or a whaler. The most common examples are decorations on whalebone or wooden stays (busks), used in the eighteenth and nineteenth centuries to reinforce women's corsets. Often given as gifts, busks were carved with dates, initials, and tokens of love—the most prevalent one being a heart or a pair of hearts. These tended to be explicit. One French-made busk engraved with two adjacent hearts noted "LA'MOUR LES JOINT" (*Figure 24*). In another French version the donor addresses the busk, "You will be there the day and I shall be there the night."[26] Other examples, one labeled "E A 1786," showed two hearts touching each other at their ends (*Figure 25*); another was engraved with two superimposed hearts and the date 1777 (*Figure 26*). Already common in eighteenth-century Europe, these expressions of love's union appeared regularly in New England. A 1782 busk, reportedly found in Strafford, Vermont (*Figure 27*), includes a message encircling two adjacent hearts: "If U Love Me As I Love U Then I & U Will Make 1 of 2." A similar posy is inscribed on the underside of an eighteenth-century New England patch box.[27]

After 1780 this popular concept of conjugal love was enshrined in some American communities by the overriding revolutionary spirit that gave commonplace symbols a new universal meaning. When late eighteenth-century calligraphers, amateur artists, and academy needlework teachers began to create family registers for private display, they drew on traditional European, Mediterranean, and Asian genealogical emblems—the biblical or genealogical family "tree"—while also adding to the design the more popular tandem, doubled, or superimposed hearts. The motive of these teachers was probably both artistic and commercial since the records would promote their professions. After all, what large and successful families would not hope to celebrate their marriages with commissioned pieces? But instructors also passed on drawing and embroidery techniques to a younger generation who went on to sketch, paint, and stitch genealogical records to give to their parents, their grandparents, and their own progeny.

In New England this process succeeded in bringing life and vibrant color into what had long been a prosaic occupation. Family information—such as a first marriage, a second or third marriage, a new birth, or even a recent death—that previously had been "concealed" within a Bible or a graveyard now became part of the newly visible family record. This mixing of popular art and decorative color had long characterized the work of Fraktur artists immigrating to Pennsylvania and Maryland who brought these ideas with them from Germany. The same combination was now flourishing in an English-speaking culture and represented a resurgence of old images in a new and dynamic social context. This impetus to create "American" decorated family records soon took on a life of its own—in effect becoming an American innovation that temporarily united popular and traditional art. While leading European gentry were still grounding their genealogies (and lines of succession) with coats of arms and miniature portraiture, a few geographically isolated New England families were beginning to nourish their "fruits of Love" on crisscrossing vines and trees rooted in a pair of overlapping hearts.

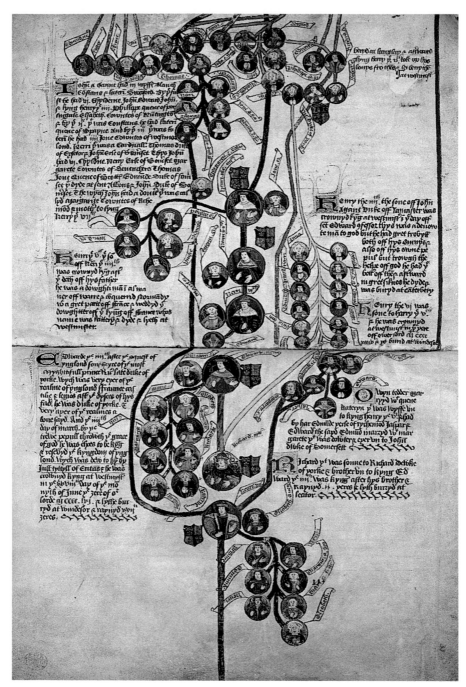

Figure 12. Detail. "Biblical and genealogical chronicle from Adam and Eve to Edward VI." Watercolor. London or Westminster, U.K., circa 1511 with additions before 1553. 34 pages. © The British Library, King's 395 f. 33.

Fruits of the Tree of Life

Figure 13. "The Progenie of Geffrey Chaucer." John Speed (1552?–1629), frontispiece in Thomas Speght, *The Workes of our antient and lerned English Poet, Geffrey Chaucer.* London: Adam Islip, 1598. Used by permission of the Folger Shakespeare Library.

Figure 14. Richard Brathwaite, *The English Gentleman and English Gentlewoman Both in one Volume couched*. London: John Dawson, 1641. Detail of title page. Courtesy of the Boston Public Library.

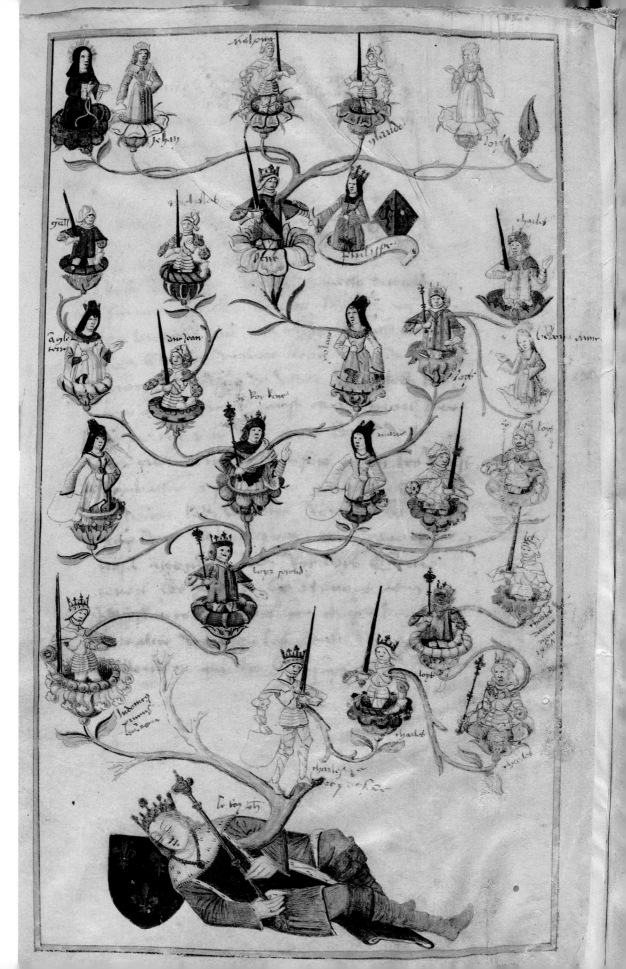

Figure 16. "Genealogia divi beinrici imperatoris." Illustration of the genealogy of the Holy Roman Emperor showing lifelines traveling female to female. From the *Nuremberg Chronicle* by Hartmann Schedel (1440–1514). Published 1493 in Nuremberg by Anton Koberger. Bavarian State Library. World Digital Library.

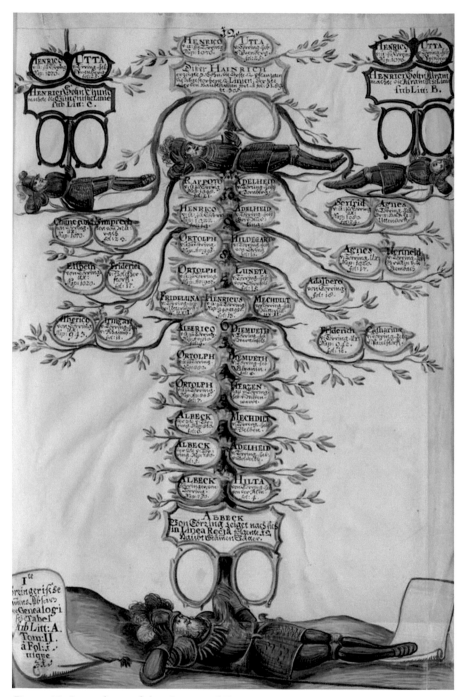

Figure 17. Genealogy of the Counts of Törring, Bavaria, circa 1724. Johann Michael Wilhelm von Prey zu Strasskirchen (1690–1747), compiler. From the Collection on the Genealogy of Bavarian Nobility, Volume 27. Bavarian State Library. World Digital Library.

(right page) Figure 18. "Stammbaum der Familie Bach, Ohrdrufer Linie" ("Family Tree of the Bach Kindred, Ohrdruf Branch"), circa 1773. Staatsbibliothek, Berlin, Germany.

Fruits of the Tree of Life

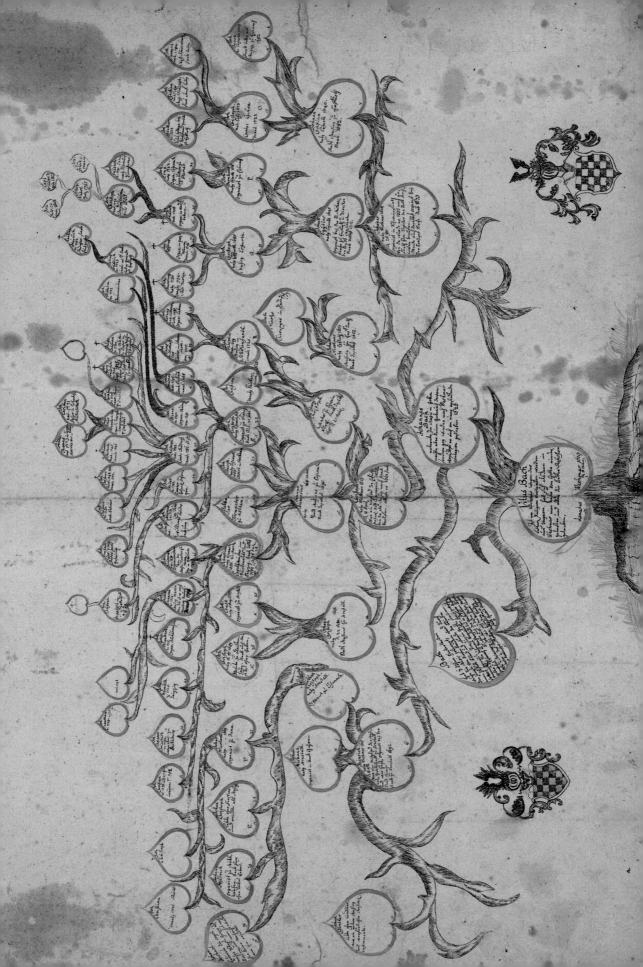

D.ᵃ Bar
the Cor
dero.

D.ᵃ Fran
Gomez.

D.ᵈᵒⁿ
ádoardo.

D.ᵃ Ana
M.ᵃᵈᵒⁿᵃ

D. Gomes
Joanes.

D.ᵃ Úrsula
Caleinas.

D.ⁿ Juan
Cordero.

D.ᵃ Catha
lina Ponce.

D.ⁿ Gregorio
Odoardo Ayud.ᵃ
de la Plaza de el
Tercio d la Artille.ᵃ
d la Ciudad d
Cadiz.

D.ᵃ Úrsola
Joanes.

D.ⁿ Joseph Cor
dero, y Ponce, Probe
edor d las Reales
Armas d S.M.ᵈ

D.ᵃ Ynes Ma
ria Odoardo, y
Joanes.

D.ⁿ Domin
go Cordero Odo
ardo, Ponce, y
Joanes.

D.
Rosa
Joseph
Anton
Co

Figure 19. Family tree showing four generations rising from the marriage of Rosa Maria and Antonio Joseph Cordero. Watercolor, 1755. Daughters of the Republic of Texas Collection at Texas A & M University, San Antonio, Texas.

Figure 20a. Schematic drawing of an English gold posy ring with twin-hearts inscribed on the inside. Attributed to Henry Bance, London, circa 1706–1721. British Museum, 1961.1202.216.

Figure 20b. Schematic drawing of an English (?) gold and enameled mourning ring with twin heart inscription on the inside. 1714. British Museum, AF.1602. Bequeathed by Sir Augustus Wollaston Franks.

Figure 21. Four views of a French posy ring decorated with multiple sprigs and a heart; "pence de moy" written on outside. Gold. France or England, circa 1400–1450. Victoria and Albert Museum, M.222.1962. Gift of Dame Joan Evans.

Figure 22. Heart-shaped locket reputedly designed to hold a child's caul. Made for the birth of John Monson of England in 1597. Gold with black enamel. Victoria and Albert Museum, M.28-1981.

Figure 23. Schematic drawing of a double-heart mourning pendant made for 33-year-old Eliphal Allen, wife of Z. Allen. Scrimshaw. England or America, 1807.

Figure 24. Detail. Scrimshaw busk. "LA' MOUR LES JOINT." France, seventeenth century. Metropolitan Museum of Art, 30.135.20.

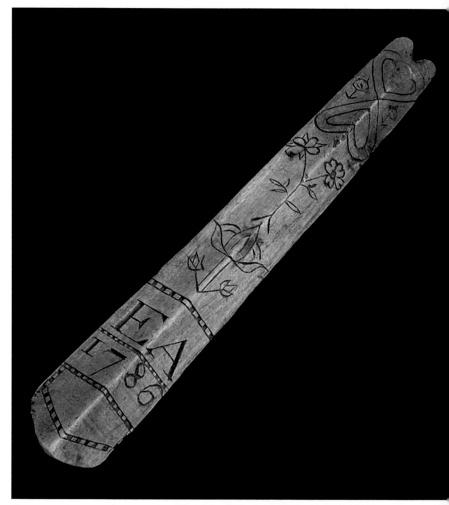

Figure 25. Decorated wooden busk showing two hearts touching at the ends. "E A" has not been identified. Probably English or French, 1786. Photograph courtesy of Shaw Edwards Antiques, Berkshire and Devon, U.K.

Figure 26. Detail. Wooden busk showing superimposed hearts and engraving of a ship. English or American, 1777. Photograph courtesy of Lyashenkoks, AncientPoint.com.

Figure 27. Detail. Busk, Strafford, Vermont, dated 1782. Wood. Winterthur Museum, 1992.87.

Figure 28 [checklist 1]. Zaccheus Coffin / Thankful Joy memorial and family tree. Signed: "Nantucket Drawn by Phebe Folger." Watercolor. Nantucket, Massachusetts, circa 1788. Courtesy of the Nantucket Historical Association, 1927.28.1. Gift of Grace Brown Gardener.

Fruits of the Tree of Life

The Hearts-and-Vines Variants
on Nantucket Island and Martha's Vineyard

The twin-heart motif appears almost simultaneously in three geographic areas of concentration in late eighteenth- and early nineteenth-century Massachusetts. These locations are Nantucket Island and Martha's Vineyard; Gloucester's Fifth Parish (now the town of Rockport); and eastern Middlesex County (primarily the towns of Lexington, Waltham, and Watertown). We do not know where the motif first started, however, but one possibility may have been on Nantucket Island in 1788 or 1789, or about six years before Edward D. Burke made the Marshall/Burnell piece. No conclusive dates can be assigned to any of these early Nantucket registers including Burke's, but the oldest in terms of style seems to be the Coffin/Joy memorial (*Figure 28*) [checklist 1] made for Zaccheus Coffin who died "in Captivity at Algiers." The memorial, owned by the Nantucket Historical Association, has a tentative design as a family tree, since the two hearts at the bottom are half buried in a small mound of green earth and each nourishes a vine-like flowering tendril. Zaccheus Coffin and Thankful Joy's two children, Bethiah and Zaccheus, however, are suspended in air just below two large rose blossoms with no vines or tendrils reaching them. Significantly, the document was signed by Phebe Folger (1771–1857), the daughter of an educated and highly prolific Nantucket family who may have played a major role in initiating the twin-heart motif on the two islands. In the following year Folger also produced a Coffin coat of arms signed "Phebe Folger / 1789" in the lower right-hand corner, demonstrating that at the age of 18 she was already a gifted designer capable of intricate calligraphy.[28]

A likely companion to the Coffin/Joy memorial is the anonymous Gardner/Beard family tree (*Figures 29 and 30*) [checklist 2], a watercolor also owned by the Nantucket Historical Association, displaying two crossing vines growing from a pair of hearts. The names of ten children born to Ebenezer Gardner Jr. and Ruth Beard between 1752 and 1770 are written on symmetrical red-rimmed pods or ovals placed close to the rising vines. Like the Coffin/Joy memorial, the design seems tentative. The ten pink-colored rose blossoms, which presumably represent these ten children, are not graphically linked

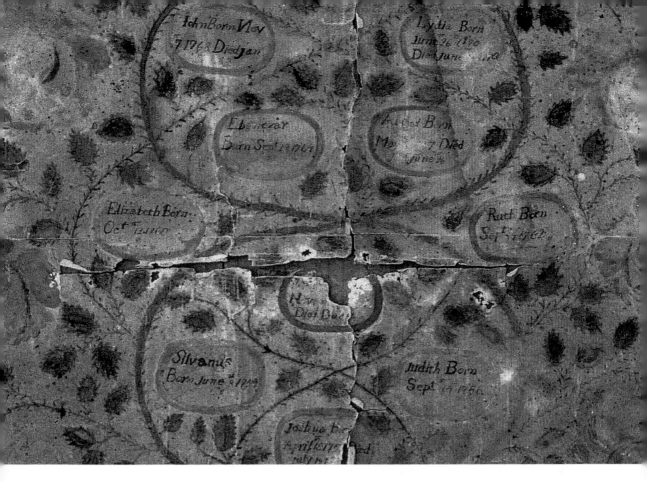

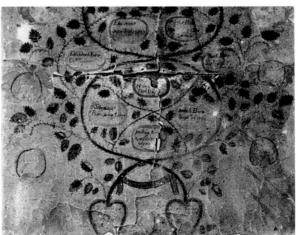

Figures 29 and 30 [checklist 2]. Two details. Ebenezer Gardner / Ruth Beard family tree. Watercolor. Nantucket, Massachusetts, circa 1788. Courtesy of the Nantucket Historical Association, 1932.30.2. Gift of William F. Macy from the Estate of Lizzie Macy.

to them, although they are nourished on the vines themselves. The surrounding foliage has a "primitive" appearance that captures the untamed quality of the low-lying salt-spray rose bushes on which they seem to be based. (These plants grow wild on the islands off Cape Cod, but they may also have been cultivated.) Nor is there any sign that the painter and calligrapher—who misspelled at least one of the names ("Ebenezar" for Ebenezer) and "marid" for "married" and who made the "N" in "Nov[ember]" backward—had any substantial academic or technical training. Perhaps the artist had been enrolled at a grammar school or academy in Nantucket where the pupils were instructed in lettering, penmanship, and painting in watercolors, or he or she may have been a teacher-in-training there.

We learn more about Phebe Folger's life both as an artist and as the wife of a Nantucket whaling captain when we examine her commonplace book, now at the Houghton Library at Harvard University.[29] "Un Recueil: Containing Painting, Penmanship, Algebra and Pieces selected from various Authors . . . By Phebe Folger," a 139-page manuscript, made during the years from 1797 to 1806, contains a number of drawings, watercolors, poems, translations, and calligraphic styles (*Figure 31*). It reveals not only that this talented young watercolorist studied English and French classics but also that she enjoyed a theoretical mind, which enabled her to learn mathematics. Most revealing for our purposes, though, are the drawings of the *Rosa rugosa,* or salt-spray rose (*Figure 32*), which match what remains of the images of this pink flower found on the Gardner/

Figure 31 (top). Watercolor drawing of pink flowers. Phebe Folger, "Un Recueil: Containing Painting, Penmanship, Algebra and Pieces selected from various Authors." Nantucket, Massachusetts, 1797 to 1806.

Figure 32 (bottom). Watercolor illustration of *Rosa Rugosa* or Salt Spray Rose. Phebe Folger, "Un Recueil . . . ." Nantucket, Massachusetts, 1797 to 1806.

Beard piece, especially where the petals are marked off by a dark circle at the base of each flower, but also in the evenly spaced thorns bordering the leaves and stems. These details argue that both early pieces were created in the immediate household of the Walter and Elizabeth Folger family itself where Phebe was the principal artist.

The key question is this: if Edward D. Burke did not bring the twin-heart motif with him from Ireland, where did Phebe Folger (or for that matter any other Nantucket artist or calligrapher) obtain it? Images of twin hearts were widely available to early nineteenth-century islanders and other maritime communities in southern New England and may have been accessible much earlier. In addition to rings, they are also seen on valentines, on carved busks, and on other local vernacular accessories. The most significant of these is the twin-heart image sprouting two intertwining flowering rose vines found on an engraved and painted busk in the collection of the New Bedford Whaling Museum (*Figure 33*).[30] The emblem is virtually the same as the Nantucket one, except that it was made much later and in this case an arrow pierces the two hearts. Numerous other heart-decorated busks, some with associated vines and trees, are found in the collection of the Nantucket Historical Association, including at least one from the eighteenth century.[31]

Other more sophisticated elements of the Nantucket twin-heart design, however, may have simply derived from a chance visit of a neighbor or a seaman who had seen a genealogical design in his or her travels elsewhere in the United States or in Europe—or from printed sources, perhaps inspired by Phebe Folger's visits to a private library or to a Boston book dealer. Was Phebe aware that some Fraktur artists used the heart-within-heart design on family records in Pennsylvania and Maryland?[32] Did she know that the curved green earth into which she planted the hearts representing Zaccheus Coffin and Thankful Joy were part of a centuries-long symbolic European tradition of stitching genealogical roots in crewel work and coverlets?

Figure 33. Busk. Whalebone, engraved with hard paint. Twin-heart growing two intertwining roses. Anchor at bottom. Height: 12 ⅞ in. North America, early nineteenth century. Courtesy of the New Bedford Whaling Museum, 1948.30.206.

The eighteenth-century women of the town of Castelo Branco in Portugal had for years embroidered coverlets (*Figure 34*) and tapestries with tree-of-life images growing on similar mounds—some resembling piles of stone—and hung them from windows once or twice each year to celebrate their families. While their makers did not expect their coverlet designs to influence English speakers on Nantucket, it is entirely possible a passing Nantucket seaman transmitted the idea to an artistically inclined woman after his return to the island.[33]

Print sources may also be responsible for the regular patterned crisscrossing of the rose vine, the concept of showing children's births as flowers, and the use of hearts to represent parents—all of which are found on genealogical imprints that gained wide circulation in London and may have reached New England. One possible source may have been Benjamin Wright's 1603 "The Roiail Progenei of our Most Sacred King Iames" (*Figure 35*)—an engraving most likely based on a circa 1603 painting—where the flowering vine of the original ancestors is shown growing in a mound of earth, the mound serving as a substitute of a deceased ancestor. That same symbol of generation is repeated on coats of arms shown on either side of the images depicting Henry VII and his wife Elizabeth. Another was the "Arbor coniugales Genealogiae Iacobi VI" of 1603 to 1612 (*Figure 36*). Here the royal succession begins with a heart-shaped medallion bearing a double coat of arms before rising into the named roundels of their progeny which are marked by the characteristic crowns (the reigns) and clasping hands (marriages). Perhaps the most compelling print is John Goddard's remake of Richard Dey's original image, "The Tree of Mans Life" (*Figure 37*), a 1639 to 1650 emblematic composition which shows two vines crossing and recrossing as they grow, leaving branches with all of the stages of men's and women's lives: birth, sustenance, burial, resurrection, and reward. While a direct tie between these early Nantucket attempts cannot be made to the medieval-period prone bodies of Henry III and Edward IV in whose abdomens the vines and "flowering" effigies were planted or to their calligraphic conceits and witticisms (like miniature frames joining hands with one another to show marriages), it seems evident that both the eighteenth- and nineteenth-century artists and the amateur calligraphers on Nantucket wanted to express the same idea: that children are the product of conjugal love.[34]

The possible existence of a Nantucket school that included a calligraphy and watercolor curriculum reinforces this connection. Five surviving Nantucket-type family registers have enough characteristics in common to suggest that the Folger household was not only involved in the creation of the original genealogical version of the twin-heart concept on the island, but also in the possible founding of a homeschool or academy that taught the style to others. These registers are the superbly executed Folger/Starbuck (*Figure 38*) [checklist 3] and Folger/Folger (*Figure 39*) [checklist 13] family trees in which Phebe and Phebe's younger sister Rebecca (1778–1823) are shown as siblings in the first, and Rebecca as a mother of five children in the second. These have variously been attributed to Phebe Folger and to Rebecca Folger,[35] shown here in a profile image dated in the early nineteenth century (*Figure 40*). Another in the same manner was painted by John Brown Copp of Stonington, Connecticut (*Figure 41*) [checklist 4], in about 1810 to 1815. A fourth was a watercolor attributed to Sarah Rodman of New Bedford and the Sherborn district in Nantucket (*Figure 42*) [checklist 10] in about 1810. A contemporary notation in the upper left-hand corner ("Not correct") was probably a teacher's comment or summation of the piece. A fifth example was a watercolor register (*Figure 43*) [checklist 14] made out for the 1770 marriage of Nantucket residents Edward Cary and Lydia Barnard and their ten children, which has been tentatively dated between 1800 and 1815. Seemingly later in style because of the manner of lightly shading the backside of leaves and of rooting the adjacent bushes on either side of the hearts, the Cary/Barnard piece nevertheless has most of the characteristics of this type. All five of them display identical triple- or double-crossed stem designs and relatively precise upper- and lowercase lettering as well as the traditional patch of earth supporting their hearts and identical twin vines. More important, they have in common a number of flower types that follow Phebe's style of watercolor illustration seen in her copybook, such as the distinctive salt-spray rose, but also a variety of local blossoms (pinks, woodbines, bluebells, lilies). We can well imagine a more mature Phebe Folger composing these family trees—or for that matter, Phebe guiding Rebecca as a pupil in her school to create one of them for their mother and father and one for Rebecca's own family after Rebecca's marriage to Alexander Folger in 1800. We can also imagine John Brown Copp learning this style during a visit to Nantucket in 1800, as well as Sarah Rodman and other younger watercolorists attending such a school after her family had moved from Nantucket to New Bedford in 1789.

The Coffin/Joy, Gardner/Beard, and the five Nantucket "school" watercolors are early examples of a precisely defined group of family registers with a Nantucket or a Martha's Vineyard history, many preserved at the Nantucket Historical Association, though some are also in private ownership or held by dealers or collectors. They identify a regional style followed on the two islands in the period from about the late 1780s through approximately 1881. Two principal variants seem to have emerged. In the first, the rose stems cross each other two or three times as they ascend, leaving at least three tiers of names—the older children appearing at the bottom. (This was adequate to represent the number of children in most families.) Names of the parents are written on the hearts, with their marriage date suspended on ribbons attached just above the hearts. Sometimes the stems and leaves are covered with thorns, as on the 1788 Gardner/Beard watercolor and later registers, such as Pent/Ripley (*Figure 44*) [checklist 15], Myrick/Mitchell (*Figure 45*) [checklist 17], and Coffin/Swain (*Figure 46*) [checklist 20]. In others the stems and branches are bare as they are in the

Folger/Coffin family tree (*Figure 47*) [checklist 16]. The pods holding the nametags continue to be disassociated from the surrounding rose blossoms but near enough to them to serve the purpose of identifying their exact parentage. Deaths are shown by a broken stemmed rose pointing down and turning brown and a mourning dove holding one end of a banner announcing the date.

As the motif evolved on the islands, a second variant emerged that also involved interlacing stems of wild roses. In these records, the names of children are integrated into the flower itself, usually on a part of the stamen or filament rather than on the petals of the blossom. This technique is best illustrated by the three Nantucket pieces by Edward D. Burke. Hiller/Smith (*Figure 48*) [checklist 5], Marshall/Burnell (*Figures 1 and 2*) [checklist 6], and Wood/Tupper (*Figure 49*) [checklist 7] all have in common a finished and professional look; all are individually signed, and all follow the same crossed-vine formula and the distinctive five-petal rose blossoms. The parents' names are written directly on the stems of the vines; the names of children are inserted in the circular husk above each flower. But because none of the parents was related to Burke, the likelihood is that they were commissioned pieces sought by parents or other relatives expecting a coherent statement about their families from a professional family register artist. Burke, who composed precise set pieces, seems to have been the only artist in this medium who had some measure of artistic training.

A possible student or assistant to Burke may have been a young Rhode Island-born teacher named Daniel Stanton who is known from two family registers. The first was made for a family in Hopkinton, Rhode Island (Kinyon/Westcott, *Figure 50*) [checklist 9]. It is unusual in several ways, since it features what appear to be national or family emblems (an American eagle and letter "S") and because each flower is split in half to create a pair of upside-down hearts. It also is an off-island version of the Nantucket type, one of only three now known. The second Stanton piece celebrates the Nantucket family of Crispus Gardner and Margaret Chase (*Figure 51*) [checklist 11] where Stanton was presumably teaching school. Both examples were signed by Daniel Stanton and both resemble Burke's in most ways.

Related to these Burke or Stanton pieces, though not part of them, is what appears to be a homemade family tree, one of the most compelling examples of the Nantucket/Martha's Vineyard group. The Gardner/Paddack (Paddock), Cartwright/Bunker, and Cartwright/Gardner family tree (*Figure 52*) [checklist 8] uses similar five-petal roses and parents' names written on the rose stems to document a sequence of marriages integrating three Nantucket families noted for their engagement with the sea. The design consists of three tandem marriage trees. First is Peter Gardner's espousal to Abigail Paddack in 1776; second is Benjamin Cartwright's union to Elisabeth Bunker in 1772; and third is widower Benjamin Cartwright's union to the widowed Abigail Paddack Gardner in 1788. Drawn and signed in 1796 by a close family relative (Eunice Gardner, Benjamin's niece and first cousin to Abigail), this piece is unique among New England marriage registers because it identifies and brings together the progeny from one of two earlier unions to form a third family. With roots of all three families planted firmly in the same curved green-colored earth, the parents of the third union (that between Abigail Paddack Gardner and Benjamin Cartwright) are depicted presiding over a family of five stepchildren (aged between 21 and 12 years of age), four of their own children (aged between 8 and 1), and the memory of four deceased children and stepchildren. Details of Eunice Gardner's image depict a partnership of families decimated by the maritime deaths that characterized so much of the islands' life in the eighteenth and nineteenth centuries. This was not only true of Eunice's own family; her father Barnabas Gardner "died at sea in the war" and her brother Barnabas Gardner Jr. was "lost at sea." It was also true of the three families she portrayed. Elizabeth Bunker's father David was "lost at sea" (in Indonesia) in 1755, David's 22-year-old grandson William Bunker, together with his mother's first cousin once removed (20-year-old David Cartwright), were "Lost at Sea 1792" or "Lost with William Bunker" in the same accident.[36] All told, at least sixty-seven Nantucket men whose surnames were Cartwright, Bunker, or Gardner died at sea before 1850. The entire toll of maritime deaths in Nantucket and Martha's Vineyard was staggering.

This demographic pattern may explain why a genealogical coding system that allowed compounded marriages to be readily added to an image flourished in Nantucket. Another triple union is illustrated by the three marriages of Nathaniel Starbuck to Eunice Barnard in 1765, to Salley Fullenton in 1777, and to Patience Coffin in 1778 (*Figure 53*) [checklist 12]. This design conforms to the island's usual symbols by designating births with lively flowers and deaths with withered husks, but because Starbuck was the father of all the children in this record, his name is shown only once—displayed on a ribbon before the tree. His three wives, however, are represented by a single heart at the base. The Starbuck register is signed "E 1812" with the initial enlarged. Because some elements of the painting style are similar to three coat-of-arms images in the Nantucket Historical Association collection, one of which is signed by Eunice Gardner, it is possible this was also her work.

A late manifestation of the island style is a family tree, donated in 2003 to the collection of the Nantucket Historical Association, that depicts children through the intertwining of two strawberry plants instead of the usual pair of salt-spray roses. Possibly done as late as 1831, the customary two hearts are embedded in a mound of blue earth; a crisscrossing vine is hung with strawberries, smaller vines, and leaves; and suspended in between them are nine circular fruits naming the children from the marriage of Samuel Coffin (1746–1809) and Eunice Folger (1754–1838) (*Figure 54*) [checklist 18]. A second piece in the same strawberry style [checklist 22], said to have been done in 1881,[37] is a partial copy of the first with three additional marriages higher up in the image.

Figure 34. Castelo Branco coverlet showing a tree of life growing in a curved earth mound. 86 x 70 ½ in. Portugal, eighteenth century. Photograph courtesy of Cora Ginsburg, *Costume, Textiles, and Needlework,* 2008.

Figure 35. Benjamin Wright, "The Roiail Progenei of our Most Sacred King Iames by the grace of God . . . ." showing the present king's line of succession from Henry Lancaster. Published by John Woutneel, 1603; second state by Compton Holland, 1619. © National Portrait Gallery, London, NPG D1370.

Fruits of the Tree of Life

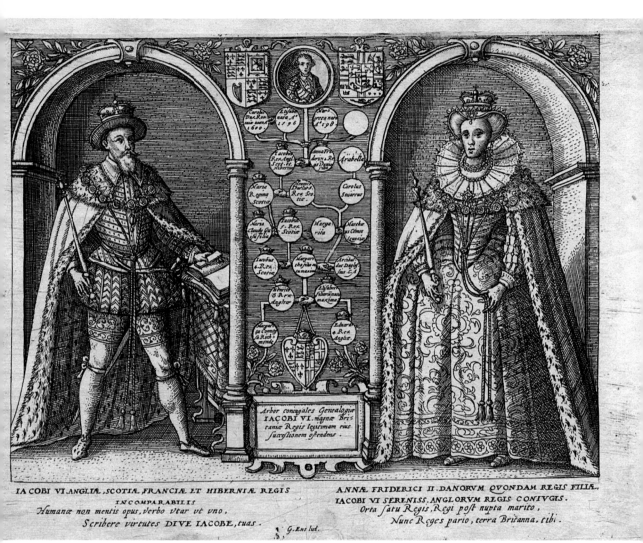

Figure 36. "Arbor coniugales Genealogiae IACOBI VI. magnae Britaniae Regis legitimam eius successionem ostendens." Etching, 1603–1612. © National Portrait Gallery, London, NPG D18233.

Figure 37. John Goddard, "The Tree of Mans Life Or an Emblem declaring the like, and unlike, or various condition of all men in their estate of Creation, birth, life, death, buriall, resurrection, and last Judgment . . ."; after Richard Dey (1559). Engraved print. London, 1639–1650. Courtesy National Gallery of Art, Rosenwald Collection, 1950.17.85.

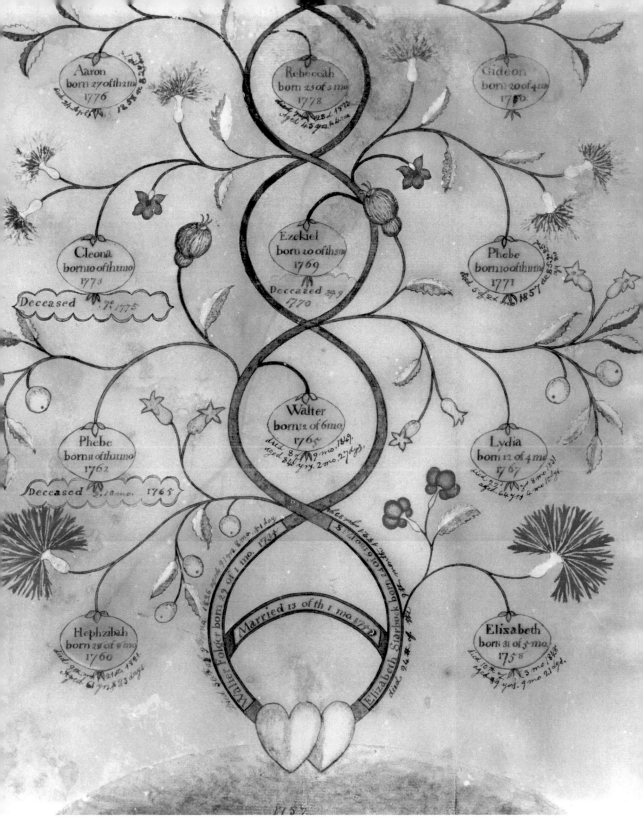

Figure 38 [checklist 3]. Walter Folger / Elizabeth Starbuck family tree. Watercolor. Nantucket, Massachusetts, circa 1789–1800. Courtesy of the Nantucket Historical Association Research Library, 1905.29.2. Gift of Jane L. Folger.

Figure 39 [checklist 13]. Alexander Folger / Rebecca Folger family tree. Watercolor. Courtesy of the Nantucket Historical Association Research Library, 1905.29.1. Gift of Jane L. Folger.

Fruits of the Tree of Life

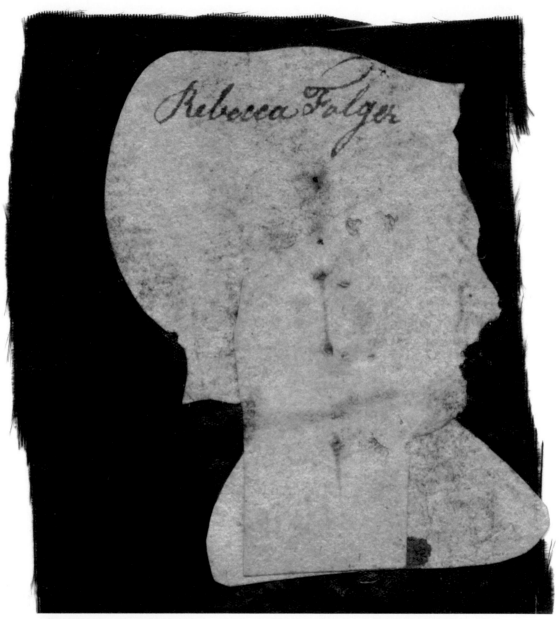

Figure 40. Rebecca Folger (1778–1823). Profile image. Nantucket, Massachusetts, early nineteenth century. Paper applied to silk. Height 2 ½ inches, length 1 ¾ inches. Courtesy of the Nantucket Historical Association Research Library, 1895.47.9.

Figure 41 [checklist 4]. Samuel Copp / Dolley Brown family tree. "John B. Copp Pinxit."
Watercolor. Stonington, Connecticut, or Nantucket, Massachusetts, circa 1810–1815.
Division of Cultural and Community Life, National Museum of American History,
Smithsonian Institution, 28810. Gift of John Brenton Copp.

Fruits of the Tree of Life

Figure 42 [checklist 10]. Samuel Rodman / Elizabeth Rotch family tree.
Attributed to Sarah Rodman (1793–1888). Watercolor. New Bedford or Nantucket,
Massachusetts, circa 1810. Formerly the property of Brian and Pamela Ehrlich.

Figure 43 [checklist 14].
Edward Cary / Lydia
Barnard family tree.
Watercolor. Nantucket,
Massachusetts, circa
1800–1815.

Figure 44 [checklist 15]. Samuel Pent /
Deborah Ripley family tree. Watercolor.
Martha's Vineyard, Massachusetts, circa
1823–1830. Ex collection Pam Boynton.

Figure 45 [checklist 17]. George Myrick Jr. /
Eliza Mitchell family tree. Watercolor.
Nantucket, Massachusetts, circa 1829.
Courtesy of the Nantucket Historical
Association Research Library, 1925.8.20.
Gift of Mary L. Myrick Fuller.

Figure 46 [checklist 20]. William Barnard Coffin /
Deborah Swain family tree. Maker unknown.
Watercolor. Nantucket or Martha's Vineyard,
Massachusetts, circa 1830–1835. Private collection.

The Hearts-and-Vines Variants on Nantucket Island and Martha's Vineyard 49

Figure 47 [checklist 16]. Charles Folger / Judith Coffin family tree. Watercolor. Nantucket, Massachusetts, circa 1827. Photograph courtesy of Pook and Pook, Inc.

Fruits of the Tree of Life

Figure 48 [checklist 5]. Thomas Hiller / Elizabeth Smith family tree. Signed: "Edw.ᵈ D. Burke, Pinxit." Watercolor. Nantucket, Massachusetts, circa 1794–1795. Courtesy of the Nantucket Historical Association Research Library, 1968.10.6. Gift of Florence and Grace Bolles.

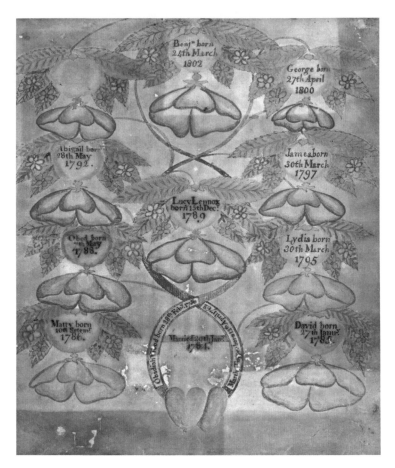

Figure 49 [checklist 7].
Obadiah Wood /
Martha Tupper
family tree. Signed:
"Edw'd. D. B[urke]."
Watercolor. Nantucket,
Massachusetts, circa
1797–1802. Private
collection.

Figure 50 [checklist 9]. John Stanton
Kinyon / Hannah Westcott family tree.
"Drawn by Daniel S. Stant[on] 1796."
Watercolor. North Kingston, Rhode Island,
1796. Location unknown. Sold by Garth's
Auctioneers and Appraisers, 2010.

Figure 51 [checklist 11]. Crispus Gardner /
Margaret Chase family tree. Signed:
"Daniel Stanton Pinxit." Watercolor.
Nantucket, Massachusetts, circa 1810–
1820. Photograph courtesy of Robert
Cary Caldwell.

Fruits of the Tree of Life

Figure 52 [checklist 8]. Combined family trees of Peter Gardner / Abigail Paddack, Benjamin Cartwright / Elizabeth Bunker, and Benjamin Cartwright / Abigail Gardner. Signed: "Dron by Eunice Gardner 1796." Watercolor. Nantucket, Massachusetts, 1796. Courtesy of the Nantucket Historical Association Research Library, 1904.35.1. Gift of Mary C. Whippey.

Figure 53 [checklist 12]. Combined family tree of Nathaniel Starbuck / Eunice Barnard / Salley Fullenton / Patience Coffin. Signed: "E 1812." Attributed to Eunice Gardner. Watercolor. Nantucket, Massachusetts, 1812. Location unknown. Photograph courtesy of Nantucket Historical Association in 1987.

Fruits of the Tree of Life

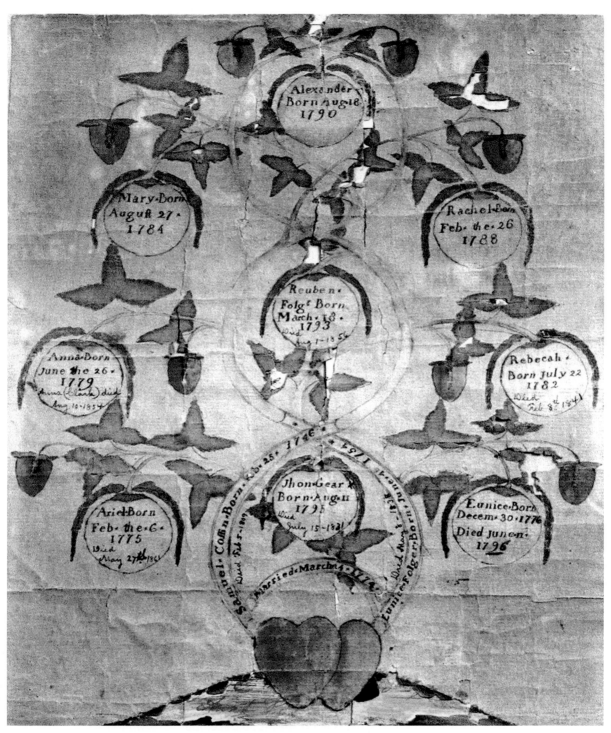

Figure 54 [checklist 18]. Samuel Coffin / Eunice Folger family tree. Watercolor. Nantucket, Massachusetts, circa 1831(?). Courtesy of the Nantucket Historical Association Research Library, 2003.23.6. Gift of Merwin Lodge.

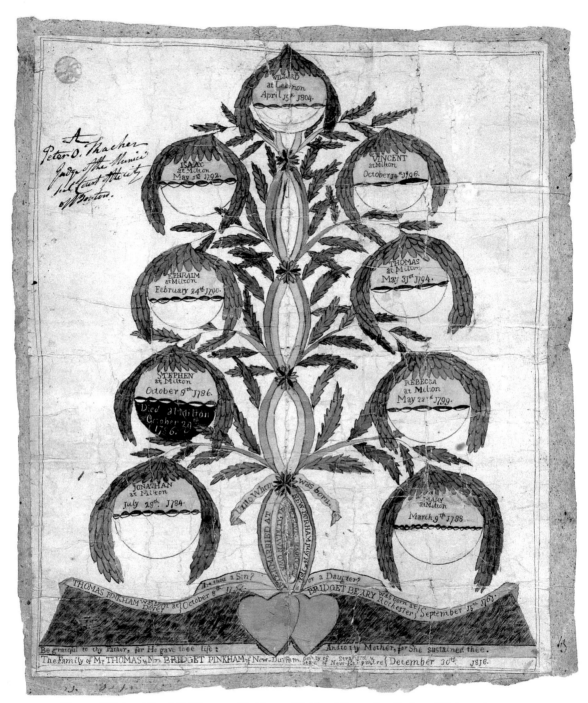

Figure 55 [checklist 23]. Thomas Pinkham / Bridget Berry family tree. Watercolor. New Durham, New Hampshire, or Lebanon, Maine, 30 December 1816. United States Revolutionary War Pension and Bounty-Land-Warrant Application Files R8260.

Fruits of the Tree of Life

"Nantucket" Variants in New Hampshire and Maine

Two watercolor family trees bearing important characteristics similar to those produced on Nantucket Island and Martha's Vineyard have been traced to inland New Hampshire and Maine communities. The records of Pinkham/Berry of New Durham, New Hampshire, and Alexander/Dicson of Webster Plantation, Maine, suggest that the hearts-and-vines motif had somehow escaped its Nantucket and Martha's Vineyard isolation and was circulating in the upper reaches of New England, almost touching the New Brunswick border with Canada. In their own way, both documents are revealing—Pinkham/Berry's because it seems like an accomplished homemade piece which precisely identifies where and when the parents and children were born; Alexander/Dicson's—a family register that was probably quickly executed—because it appears to have a very late date, perhaps in the 1840s or 1850s.[38]

The record celebrating the marriage and nine children of Thomas Pinkham and Bridget Berry (*Figure 55*) [checklist 23], a document now housed in the Revolutionary War Pension and Bounty-Land-Warrant Application Files,[39] indicates the first eight children were born in Milton, New Hampshire; the ninth child, Willard Pinkham, was born in Lebanon, Maine. These two communities adjoin one another along the states' borders, lying just north of Rochester and Portsmouth, and both are readily accessible to the sea. The Pinkham/Berry vines stand erect and are arranged like a Christmas tree, holding nine circular, unidentifiable fruits; a death is marked in black in the lower half of one fruit. The leaves are almost fernlike and clasp each fruit or ball securely.[40]

The record depicting the marriage of Thomas Alexander and Betsey Dicson and celebrating their eight children (*Figure 56*) [checklist 24] looks much like a stylized version of the Pinkham/Berry motif. It uses eight large fruits which are also tightly held by leaves that droop down like a periwig. The presence of unpainted areas around each fruit suggests that this copy was one of many and was made quickly, and in fact it may have been a duplication of an earlier family register that is now unknown. Genealogical research indicates the Alexanders lived in a community in Penobscot County approximately 250 miles away from Lebanon near the New Brunswick border. An older child was born in 1798; a son Thomas was born in "Webster Plantation" in 1809, three decades before the town was incorporated in 1840; another son, Horatio Nelson, was born in 1818; a daughter Susan was born in 1815. Like the Pinkham/Berry family tree, the Alexander/Dicson watercolor records parents on the stems of the vine and suspends the children from individual branches; one child who died the same year he was born has been separated from the tree. But Webster Plantation's geography is different. Unlike Milton and Lebanon, the community did not enjoy ready access to the sea and did not have ready access to Nantucket.[41]

Despite stylistic similarities between these two northern variants and the Nantucket / Martha's Vineyard hearts-and-vines types—usually an indication they emerged from similar origins—important differences remain. For one, both list children on large circular unidentifiable fruits, not flowers. By contrast, all twenty-two Nantucket and Martha's Vineyard vine examples carry floral or floral-related decorations such as rose blossoms, rose pods, or flower husks, and in some instances a variety of cultivated garden flowers or strawberries. Second, the New Hampshire and Maine versions have large leaves holding the fruits, and their shape is more fernlike. None of the Nantucket or Martha's Vineyard examples resembles ferns. Third, and perhaps most important, the crossing vines intersect one another four times, and each intersection is marked by a star medallion—a design feature not seen on any Nantucket or Martha's Vineyard record.

Figure 56 [checklist 24]. Thomas Alexander / Betsey Dicson family tree. Watercolor. Webster Plantation, Maine, circa 1830–1850. Location unknown. Sold by Garth's Auctioneers and Appraisers in 2016.

Figure 57 [checklist 25]. William Rowe / Betsy Dennison family tree. Signed: "William Saville Glocester [*sic*] September 17[   ]." Watercolor. Gloucester, Massachusetts, circa 1793. Sandy Bay Historical Society, 637.

Fruits of the Tree of Life

The Gloucester Watercolors

The other two concentrations of the twin-heart motif are more closely associated with established schools—one that taught navigational skills and a second that served as an academy for young women. The navigational school was located in Gloucester and was founded by William Saville,[42] a schoolmaster, town clerk, and land surveyor who lived in the town's Fifth or Sandy Bay Parish, now the town of Rockport. In addition to his other duties, Saville was responsible for a number of watercolor family registers made for Rockport and Gloucester families. In about 1793, for example, he composed a register for William Rowe and Betsy Dennison (*Figure 57*) [checklist 25] which takes the form of an apple tree adorned with three upside-down hearts; twelve children are shown as fruits hanging on individual branches of the tree. This piece, owned by the Sandy Bay Historical Society, was signed by the artist and features an apple orchard to the left of the tree and a red mansard two-floor home on the right. Saville later teamed up with a genealogical artist named Joshua Pool Jr. (1787–1838),[43] the half-brother of William Saville's first wife Esther Pool. Saville also may have worked with William Richardson (born 1813?)[44] of Gloucester, very likely a former student. As he was remembered by one nineteenth-century historian, "Master Saville" initially kept school in Gloucester's First Parish in a small gambrel-roofed house on the corner of Sea Street (now Hancock Street) owned by "Aunt Mayo," who later occupied it as a grocery store.[45] He was a painstaking watercolorist (a skill which he apparently taught himself) and was known for several memorials that he made for parents of young children and for Cape Ann's maritime leaders. In a device he painted in 1800 for Hannah, the 1-year-old child of John and Esther Gott, he used about one thousand brush strokes in bright red to illustrate Hannah's tomb (*Figure 58*).[46] He applied the same painstaking detail in drawing the semicircular tomb of Capt. John Woodbury (*Figures 5 and 6*) with approximately three hundred brush strokes. Not understood is how long Saville kept up his work either as a watercolorist or as a schoolmaster. His surveying work, known from a fine 1823 draft of the training field and meetinghouse in Gloucester,[47] may have occupied much of his time in his later years.

Together, Saville, Pool, and Richardson are responsible for nineteen known family registers. All three artists worked in watercolor, though Pool may also have used some appliqué elements; and all showed children as apples hanging on individual branches of a tree. Five of these nineteen are housed at the Sandy Bay Historical Society in Rockport; three are in the collection of Historic New England; two are at the Cape Ann Museum in Gloucester; and one is owned at the American Folk Art Museum in New York City. All are characterized by a tree emblazoned by a pair of upside-down hearts—a variant seemingly begun by Saville, who apparently used the device to help students draw with a compass and a straight edge, make letters, and create and read maps. Where did Saville learn to make this design? So far, the only known European antecedent was created by Matthias Buchinger (1674–1739), a German miniature artist and calligrapher who in 1727 devised a genealogical apple tree for the Banks/Montgomery family of Belfast, Ireland, identified by an ornate coat of arms attached to its base. Eight children are shown as hanging apples, and five apples remain blank. Several hearts are embedded into a border frame, but this symbol did not work into the design itself.[48] Nevertheless, it does suggest that apple-bearing trees, marked at their base with framed placards, served as a common genealogical format in eighteenth-century Europe. Elsewhere, Saville incorporated a single upside-down heart into his "Mourning Picture of Isaac Harding of Hamilton" (*Figure 59*), a memorial composed in 1801, presumably applying an existing family-tree device to a memory piece.[49]

The starting dates of the Gloucester motif are ambiguous. The oldest surviving piece in the Gloucester group apparently is Saville's Rowe/Dennison family register. This example seems the most tentative and exploratory in appearance, especially in the treatment of the hearts, which appear unpolished and clumsily shaded. The date is obscured by period framing, but it may coincide with the 1793 date of Saville's signed memento mori for the couple's daughter Betsy (*Figure 7*), also owned by the Sandy Bay Historical Society, and by the calligraphic shift after the birth of Amos Rowe in 1792. Saville was 23 years old in 1793 and seemingly had little training or experience using watercolors. In this instance, the original aesthetics of the design were later compromised when the Rowes ran out of space on it to record a twelfth child, and a family member awkwardly added a birth at the top of the tree, dating that element to after 1809. The register made for Thomas Robards and Dorcas Thurston (*Figure 60*) [checklist 26], attributed to Saville, is also part of this early period, as is the signed tree made for the family of David Lane and Hannah Marchent (*Figure 61*) [checklist 27]. A distinct daisy-like flower or nasturtium blossom accompanies each of the apples on the Robards/Thurston piece. Both exhibit foliage clustering about the base of the tree—a Saville feature which is found only on one or possibly two other early pieces. Another relatively early example was made for James Parsons who married Deborah Lane in 1768 and Patience Knights in 1785 (*Figure 129*) [checklist

28]. This register is unusual because the family is displayed on two trees standing side by side—the only known Saville watercolor in which this pattern is used. Deborah Parsons's children hang on the left tree, and Patience Parsons's children on the right tree. It has the specificity of some Nantucket registers—for example, Cartwright/ Gardner [checklist 8].

Later Saville family records include Grover/Tarr (*Figure 62*) [checklist 31] and Dennison/Griffin (*Figure 63*) [checklist 36], which are dated 6 May 1801 and 6 April 1815, respectively. In each case, the use of a third heart—mounted just above the parents at the base of the tree—shows the characteristic Saville manner of superimposing the base of this heart over the father's heart while tucking it under the mother's heart. The dates of the two earliest known Pool works are 1808 and 1811; the Richardson watercolor is dated 1838, or well after the period that Saville and Pool were active.

Fourteen of the nineteen known Gloucester pieces are signed by their maker. Nine bear William Saville's signature and are dated and four are signed by Joshua Pool Jr. and one by William Richardson. This pattern implies the artists did most of these on a commission basis, a presumption reinforced by several inscriptions left on Saville's memory pieces. Hannah Gott's memorial reads, "This Monument was drawn for the Relations of the deceased by . . . William Saville." Abagail Channel's memorial, also signed Saville, was "dedicated by her Friends and Relations."[50] Saville and Pool, in fact, seem to have made a business of creating family trees and memorial watercolors after the deaths of their fellow townsmen. Five Saville memorials are known, and three of these were accompanied at some point by family records. A sixth has Pool's signature and follows a different design. The memorial for Solomon Robbards's son Solomon (*Figure 64*) consists of a large urn supported on an engraved brick base reflecting on the "Precarious Condition of Humanity." A bluebird, a fence, and a row of trees provide a background. The researchers who collected materials for the Gloucester vital records were aware of these family records and sometimes specified them in their bibliographies. At least eighteen sources (all presumed to have been watercolor images) are cited as "family trees" in the *Gloucester Vital Records*.[51] None of these has been located, however.

Unlike the Nantucket and Martha's Vineyard watercolorists who kept an artistic distance between themselves and their subjects, Saville, Pool, and Richardson found numerous opportunities to add personal or community details to their designs. Many apparently depict the homesteads where the children grew up, including two-and-a-half-story mansions, gambrel-roof homes, or simple Gloucester-area half-houses. Joshua Pool's Bickford/Clark (*Figure 65*) [checklist 38], a superb watercolor family tree, now owned by the American Folk Art Museum in New York City, shows a complete farmyard surrounded by rock walls, wooden gates, an outhouse with a weather vane, pigsties, farm animals, a small barn, ploughs, a two-wheel horse cart, and a yoked pair of oxen. Less crowded but equally appealing are the three red-roof houses of Pool's Robbards/Brown family tree (*Figure 66*) [checklist 37] that features an unusual corner door almost next to the front door; a solitary cow and horseback rider are seen in the foreground. Saville's Channel/Burnham (*Figure 127*) [checklist 30] includes a newly planted orchard, a red fence, a white two-story house, and its proprietor surveying the scene. Saville's Griffin/Lane image (*Figure 67*) [checklist 32] illustrates a small orchard protected by an elaborate palisade fence that leads to and surrounds it. Pool's Tarr/Somes register (*Figure 68*) [checklist 34] hosts a half-house, a barn with six pigeon coves, and an ox-drawn farm cart. Richardson's Dennen/Gott family tree (*Figure 69*) [checklist 41] depicts a waterfront pier with pilings and a workhouse reached by a wooden walkway.

At least two Gloucester records drew attention to specific events in local family history. One family register attributed to Joshua Pool, Colbey/Tarr (*Figure 70*) [checklist 40], represents a frozen winter scene, presumably to reflect the Christmas Day (25 December 1816) when the marriage took place. Another, Hicks/Parsons (*Figures 71 and 72*) [checklist 33], signed by Joshua Pool, illustrates two masons completing the rebuilding of a chimney, no doubt a contemporary event taking place at the time the register was painted. Others are accompanied by memorials of one of the parents, such as on Woodbury/Lane, or scenes from Gloucester Harbor including a three-masted ship (a fourteen-gun brig) as seen on Colbey/Tarr, and a two-masted fishing smack as seen on Doyle/Clark (*Figure 73*) [checklist 39] and Parsons/Goss, Davis/Goss (*Figures 130 and 131*) [checklist 35]. Perhaps the most curious feature of this detail work, however, is architectural. Five large houses[52] are equipped with long mast-like poles fixed almost touching the clapboards, but none of them carries flags. We must assume that these were either wind-vanes or early lightning rods.

But, to a one, all Gloucester-area hearts are pictured "upside-down" and have the appearance of being "nailed" to the base of the tree like sign-posts or proclamations—though no nails or ribbons are visible. Each piece is like a genealogical afterthought entirely divorced from its surroundings, but still attached to the family homestead. The tree's roots are usually visible below the hearts. Not many differences exist between family trees by William Saville and those by Joshua Pool and William Richardson. Saville generally painted fewer landscape features than Pool, and he typically used a third upside-down heart to announce the date of the marriage. By contrast, Pool and Richardson sometimes employed a scroll of paper for the marriage information, and they were more detailed in illustrating the farming landscape and especially in depicting rocky shorelines and fishing vessels.

Figure 58. Memorial for Hannah Gott (1789–1790), the third child of John and Esther Gott. Signed: "William Saville." Watercolor. Gloucester, Massachusetts, 11 October 1800. 12 ¾ x 10 ¾ in. Formerly in the collection of Arthur B. and Sybil B. Kern, Pawtucket, Rhode Island. Image courtesy of Skinner, Inc., www.skinnerinc.com.

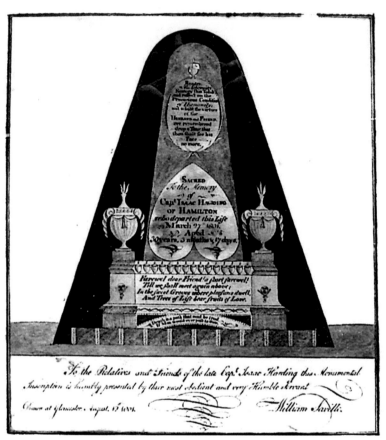

Figure 59. Memorial for Capt. Isaac Harding, Hamilton, Massachusetts. "Drawn at Gloucester August 19th 1801. William Saville." Watercolor. Photograph courtesy of Linda M. and Paul J. DeCoste, West Newbury, Massachusetts.

(right page) Figure 60 [checklist 26]. Thomas Robards [Robbins] / Dorcas Thurston family tree. Watercolor. Gloucester or Ipswich, Massachusetts, 1793[?]. Photograph courtesy of Skinner, Inc., www.skinnerinc.com.

Fruits of the Tree of Life

FAMILY RECORD.

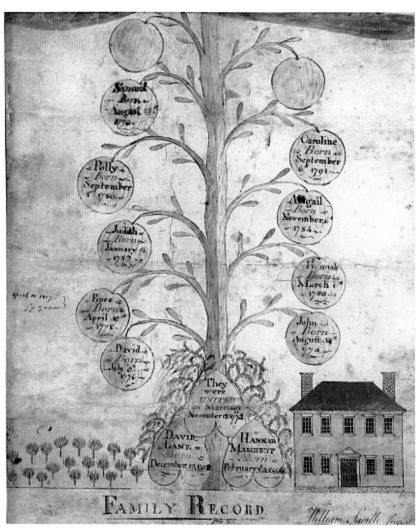

Figure 61 [checklist 27]. David Lane / Hannah Marchent family tree.
Signed: "William Saville Scripsit." Watercolor. Gloucester, Massachusetts,
1791–1793. Image taken from Schaffner and Klein, *Folk Hearts,* 56.
Ex collection Howard and Catherine Feldman.

Fruits of the Tree of Life

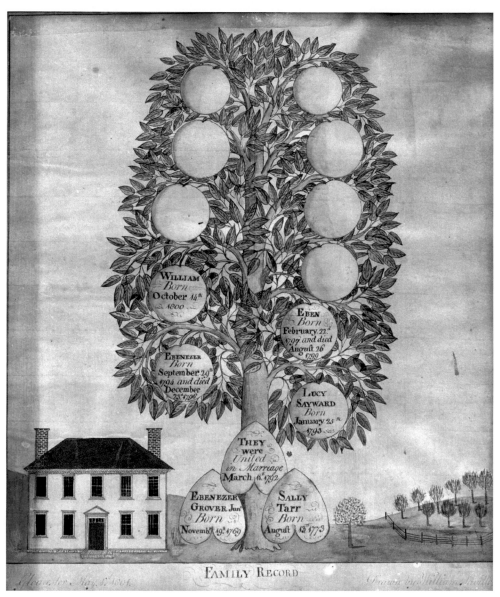

Figure 62 [checklist 31]. Ebenezer Grover / Sally Tarr family tree. Signed: "Drawn by William Saville." Watercolor. Gloucester, Massachusetts, 6 May 1801. Courtesy of Historic New England. Gift of Constance McCann Betts, Helena Woolworth Guest and Frasier W. McCann, 1942.2589.1.

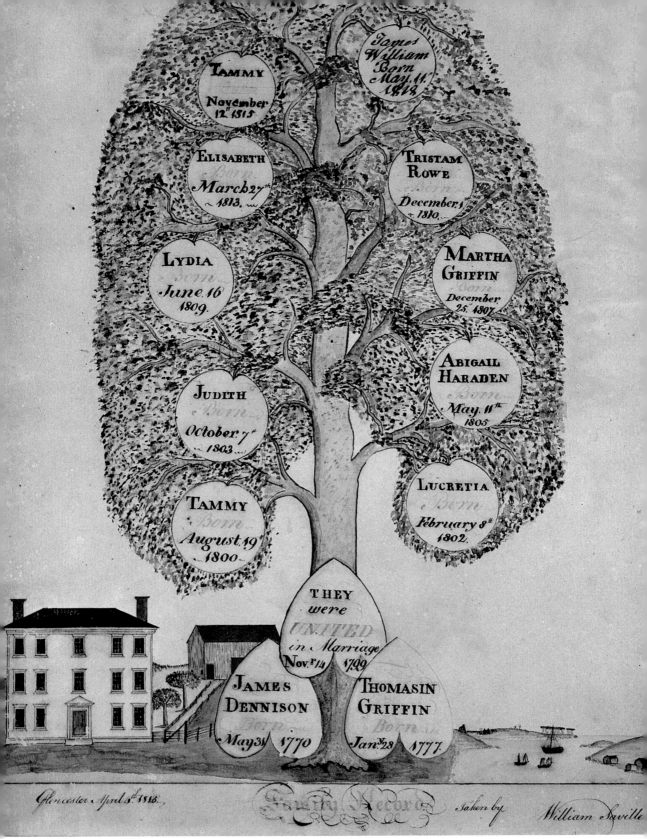

Figure 63 [checklist 36]. James Dennison / Thomasin Griffin family tree. Signed: "Gloucester April 4th 1815. Taken by William Saville." Watercolor and pen on paper. Gloucester, Massachusetts, 1815. Collection of the Cape Ann Museum.

Fruits of the Tree of Life

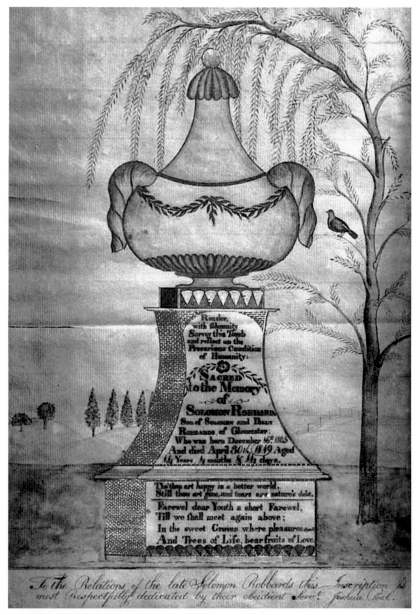

Figure 64. Memorial to Solomon Robbards, son of Solomon and Polly Robbards of Gloucester, aged 14 years. Signed: "Joshua Pool." Watercolor. 1819. Location unknown. Sold by Kaminski Auctions, 2016.

Figure 65 [checklist 38]. Andrew Bickford / Olive Clark family tree. Signed: "Done by J. Pool." Gloucester, Massachusetts, circa 1828. American Folk Art Museum, 1998.17.6. Gift of Ralph Esmerian.

Fruits of the Tree of Life

Figure 66 [checklist 37]. Solomon Robbards / Polly Brown family tree. "Drawn by J. Pool." Watercolor. Gloucester, Massachusetts, 1819. Location unknown. Sold by Kaminski Auctions, 2016.

Figure 67 [checklist 32]. Nathaniel Griffin Jr. / Priscilla Lane family tree. "Drawn by William Saville." Gloucester, Massachusetts, 1807. Sold by John McInnis Auctions, 2018.

(right page) Figure 68 [checklist 34]. Jabez Tarr / Peggy Somes family record. Watercolor. Gloucester, Massachusetts, circa 1809–1814. Sandy Bay Historical Society, 638.

Fruits of the Tree of Life

Family Record

Figure 69 [checklist 41]. Job Dennen / Lucy Gott family tree. Signed: "By Wm. Richardson." Watercolor. Gloucester, Massachusetts, 1838. Ex collection Mr. and Mrs. Erving Wolf. Image taken from Brant and Cullman, *Small Folk,* entry 70.

Figure 70 [checklist 40]. Benjamin Colbey / Lois Tarr family tree. Attributed to Joshua Pool, Jr. Watercolor. Gloucester, Massachusetts, circa 1824. Sandy Bay Historical Society, 639. Gift of Mrs. Frederick Tarr.

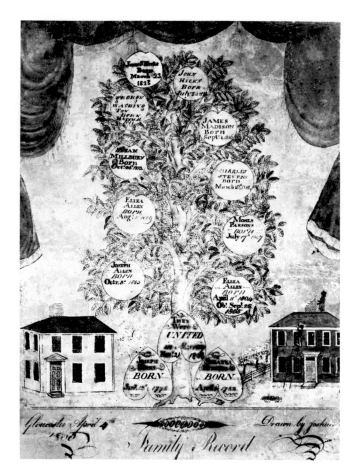

Figure 71 [checklist 33]. Joseph Hicks / Susanna Parsons family tree. Signed: "Drawn by Joshua P[ool]." Gloucester, Massachusetts, April 4, 1808. Location unknown.

Figure 72 [checklist 33]. Detail. Joseph Hicks / Susanna Parsons family tree showing masons at work on chimney.

Figure 73 [checklist 39]. Felix Doyle / Tamma Clark family tree. Attributed to Joshua Pool Jr. Watercolor. Gloucester, Massachusetts, circa 1821. Sandy Bay Historical Society, 636.

Figure 74 [checklist 44]. David Townsend / Sarah Jenison family tree. Embroidery. Middlesex County, Massachusetts (Waltham or Watertown), circa 1790. Courtesy of the Concord Museum, Gift of Russell H. Kettell. www.concordmuseum.org.

Fruits of the Tree of Life

The Middlesex County Embroideries

A third concentration of the twin-heart motif took place in one or perhaps several schools that accommodated young women in eastern Middlesex County, Massachusetts, in the period from roughly 1800 to about 1827. Taught by what is thought to be the same instructress, the embroidered designs using the motif are associated with a group of towns that include Lexington, Waltham, Watertown, Bedford, Concord, Acton, Billerica, and Woburn. They feature a pair of overlapping hearts inscribed with parental information out of which grows an apple tree bearing fruits labeled with the names and birth dates of the children. Twenty-six are known. Most are well documented with an established provenance, and twenty-three reveal the embroiderer's name and sometimes her age. A sizable number are owned by museums and historical societies: five by the Lexington Historical Society, two by the Huntington Library in San Marino, California, and one each at the Concord Museum (Massachusetts), the Winterthur Museum, the National Society of the Daughters of the America Revolution in Washington, D.C., and the DeYoung Museum in San Francisco. The remainder are owned by descendants, dealers, and private collectors. Long held by households safeguarding their relics, embroideries appear to have survived in greater numbers than watercolors and they continue to surface. Thirteen of the fifty-one new discoveries cited in the checklist are embroideries produced from the Middlesex County–area schools.

As in the case of the Nantucket / Martha's Vineyard and Gloucester groups, there is some doubt as to when this motif first appeared. The Townsend/Jenison family tree (*Figure 74*) [checklist 44], stitched on behalf of a Waltham couple, is the least developed of the twenty-six and the only example in this group that is set in an actual "landscape"—meaning that it has a horizon line. But in all the other embroideries in this series the hearts are suspended within a floral design or by ornamental leaves. This might be a sign that a different teacher was involved in the Townsend/Jenison piece, perhaps even the mentor of a younger woman who taught the more ornate examples that followed. David Townsend and Sarah Jenison had nine children born in Waltham between 1775 and 1789. If Sarah Townsend (born 1775) did the sampler, the item could date to around 1785 or 1786; on the other hand, if the embroideress was Lucy Townsend (born 1789), it could date to 1800 or later. The majority of these embroidered genealogies were stitched between the years 1807 and 1825 by girls aged 11 to 18[53] and usually by the oldest daughter in the family.

The most distinctive element of the Lexington or Middlesex County design, and one that indicates that the teacher was likely the same individual, is the characteristic shape and the coloration of the apple tree. With few exceptions, the tree trunk makes a sharp turn to the right, with the bark's being colored dark brown on one side, and then the tree switches to the left where it is colored a lighter brown or beige. The parental hearts intersect one another and are typically framed or supported in a floral swag of multicolored leaves with horizontal stripes that form a "rococo" cup or a base. Other details include apples of a different color for the boys (usually white or light beige) and girls (usually yellow or light brown)—variously seen in Russell/Blood (*Figure 75*) [checklist 55], Wellington/Ball (*Figure 76*) [checklist 47], and Stone/Coolidge (*Figure 77*) [checklist 58]. And most inscriptions abbreviate "born" as "bn." Except for the initial Townsend/Jenison piece, virtually all examples have a floral or ribbon design extending like a protective support under the tree; these embellishments sometimes are composed of linked flowers as on the Bellows/Wyeth register (*Figure 78*) [checklist 63], but some are simply repeated stitching as found on Clark/Sanderson (*Figure 79*) [checklist 48]. These features suggest that the teacher was working from a pattern book that she had created (or had purchased) and which she allowed her students to replicate.

Like the Nantucket and Gloucester genealogical types, the embroideries represent an artificial or "staged" scene where static symbols depict a succession of past events. In this case, however, the tree is "rooted" in the overlapping hearts—meaning it seems to serve the same purpose as the oval ground in the Nantucket group and the farmyard and house plots of the Gloucester group. (In the Townsend/Jenison piece, the hearts appear to be growing or sprouting up from the ground.) Many of the pieces are formally titled "Family Record" or "The Family Record" and focus on birth dates, though death dates are occasionally included. Some samplers seem to have subdued colors, perhaps those chosen by the embroiderer; others appear to have experienced fading. The Harrington/Pierce family tree (*Figure 80*) [checklist 51], completed sometime around 1810, has muted colors of yellow, deep brown, light brown, and quiet green. Colors on Mary M. Smith's Underwood/Munroe family tree (*Figure 81*) [checklist 54] seem limited to blue, dusky yellow, and brown—they are almost identical to those on Meriam/Simonds (*Figure 82*) [checklist 50]. The hues on Mulliken/Whiting (*Figure 132*) [checklist 59] are shaded yellow, brown, and green.

Figure 75 [checklist 55]. Nathan Russell / Sybil Blood family tree. "Mary Russell's Work AE 13." Embroidery. Middlesex County, Massachusetts (Lexington), 1817. Photograph courtesy of Kris Casucci.

Figure 76 [checklist 47]. Benjamin Wellington / Martha Ball family tree. Embroidery. Middlesex County, Massachusetts (Lexington), circa 1801. Courtesy of the Lexington Historical Society, 12968.

Fruits of the Tree of Life

Figure 77 [checklist 58]. William Stone / Elizabeth Coolidge family tree. "[W]rought by Elizabeth Stone 1820." Embroidery. Middlesex County, Massachusetts (Watertown), 1820. Courtesy of the Huntington Art Museum, San Marino, California.

Not all conventions were followed, however, and new ones were sometimes added. The antique dealers Stephen and Carol Huber, who have studied a number of these embroideries, point out that an early family death might be shown separated from the tree. In Plympton/Holden (*Figure 83*) [checklist 67], two apples inscribed "Louisa bn July 6 1806" and "Fanny bn Feb 24 1817" are removed from the branches, suggesting that these children did not survive—and indeed the Plympton genealogy tells us that Louisa died in 1811 and Fanny in 1821.[54] Separated apples (but not fallen ones) were symbols employed in three other Lexington or Middlesex County–area embroideries.[55] Other innovations include twins shown as two side-by-side apples on the Russell/Blood and Wellington/Ball embroideries with different colors indicating their sex: "Mary and Stephen" Russell were born on 22 February 1804; "Lydia and Sally" Russell, on 30 September 1806; "James & Patty" Wellington on 12 December 1786. But colors can be deceptive. Lorenza Fisk, who stitched a genealogy of her family in 1811 (*Figure 84*) [checklist 52], seems to have been sparing in her use of yellow silk (reserved for boys in her embroidery) since she colored a younger brother (Samuel) with the warm brownish hue reserved for girls and began a second child (Napolean) with brown and finished with yellow. Nevertheless, there is greater variety in the coloration, décor, and border designs in embroideries than is found on the watercolors made in Nantucket and Gloucester. Many of the Lexington or Middlesex County trees have two-color leaves, split down the middle with the upper halves reflecting more light. The border patterns of interlacing vines and flowers vary widely and reflect greater sophistication than the watercolors.

And there seems to have been more of a generational perspective in the Lexington embroideries than in the watercolors. In at least two instances, embroidered trees reveal a two-generation gap between the makers and their subjects. Lucebia Windship (*Figure 85*) [checklist 53] of Lexington embroidered a family tree about 1812 for her grandparents, Daniel Harrington (1739–1818) and Anna Munroe (1740–1811), whose daughter Anna Harrington married Thomas Winship of Lexington on 11 April 1793.[56] Mary M. Smith celebrated the marriage of her grandparents Joseph Underwood and Mary Munroe of Lexington, whose daughter Polly Underwood married Jonas Smith of Lexington in 1798.[57] These generational perspectives are seldom seen in Nantucket and Gloucester.

Among the last embroideries in the Lexington-area series was the Mulliken/ Reed genealogy (*Figure 133*) [checklist 68], where Susan Mulliken stitched a curved earth mound holding up the tree. This piece lacks the usual hearts—and perhaps represents a new way of thinking about the past or even a throwback to an earlier watercolor style. Another late example is the Billings/Hapgood "Family Record"

(*Figure 86*) [checklist 69] stitched in 1827 by 14-year-old Sophia Billings for her mother and father in Acton. The Billings piece has the basic appearance of earlier examples, but the emphasis is on the apples rather than the tree; it has also adopted a square format and added diamonds or zigzags to the edges of the hearts. Some of the apples have the names of two children stitched into them, each one with the individual date of birth. Missing are the two colorations of the bark and the abbreviation of "bn" for "born." These changes are clear indications that a new teacher was at work.

At least two other Massachusetts schools for young women may have introduced the twin-heart motif into their embroidery curriculum—or possibly girls were taught by mothers who encouraged the theme as a household exercise. Lucy Rice of Ashby, Massachusetts, embroidered a heart-rooted genealogical tree as a 12-year-old child [checklist 72], which is now unlocated but is known from a photograph in one of the Ethel Stanwood Bolton and Eva Johnston Coe notebooks at the Worcester Art Museum. It captures some, but not all, of the Middlesex characteristics. These include the two fronds rising from the hearts, the shape of the leaves, and the bends and coloration of the tree's trunk. But there are important exceptions. The hearts are set on a landscaped and bowered hillock; more importantly, three stanzas of poetry, three upper- and lowercase alphabets, and a row of numbers accompany her work. Although the letter "z" is backward, it seems likely she had a teacher who had at least some familiarity with the curriculum practiced there.[58]

The second example is more separated from the Middlesex group. According to the collectors Dan and Marty Campanelli, the Carver/Harlow family tree (*Figure 87*) [checklist 74][59] was produced at the Bristol Academy in Taunton sometime between 1807 and 1810. Ruth Carver, who was 14 in 1807, probably embroidered the unfinished piece whose design is dissimilar to the Middlesex County–area group: the tree is different and seems to resemble a peach; the two lower hearts are positioned "upside-down"; both hearts and fruits are edged with "fronds," and the "fruits" themselves are actually oval garlands resting lightly on the branches. Only this one example is known. The Campanellis state that Ruth Carver's instructress was likely named Miss Sally Cady, who is identified in an 1893 Taunton history as being "educated in the Capital . . . ."[60] It is unclear whether this refers to Boston, Washington, D.C., or London.

Figure 78 [checklist 63]. Samuel M. Bellows / Mary W. Wyeth family tree.
"[W]rought by Mary W. Bellows aet. 11 1821." Embroidery. Middlesex County,
Massachusetts (Arlington), 1821. Photo courtesy of Stephen and Carol Huber,
www.AntiqueSamplers.com.

Fruits of the Tree of Life

Figure 79 [checklist 48].
John Clark / Lydia Sanderson family tree.
"Alice Clark's Work." Embroidery.
Waltham, Massachusetts, circa 1807.
Photo courtesy of Stephen and Carol
Huber, www.AntiqueSamplers.com.

Figure 80 [checklist 51].
Solomon Harrington /
Hannah Pierce family tree.
"Family Record Ruth
Harringtons." Embroidery.
Waltham, Massachusetts.
Circa 1810–1815. Photo
courtesy of Stephen
and Carol Huber,
www.AntiqueSamplers.com.

Figure 81 [checklist 54]. Joseph Underwood / Mary Munroe family tree. "Mary M. Smith Work." Embroidery. Lexington, Massachusetts, circa 1810–1830. Courtesy of the Lexington Historical Society, 2546.

Fruits of the Tree of Life

Figure 82 [checklist 50]. Rufus Meriam / Martha Simonds family tree. "Eliza Meriam's Work." Embroidery. Middlesex County (Lexington), circa 1810. Courtesy of the Lexington Historical Society, 7317.

Figure 83 [checklist 67]. Thomas R. Plympton / Betsy Holden family tree. "Louisa H. Plympton." Embroidery. Middlesex County, Massachusetts (Waltham?), circa 1825–1829. Location unknown. Sold by Sotheby's in 2013, 4938, Lot 625.

Figure 84 [checklist 52]. Abraham Fisk / Grace Hagar family tree.
"Family Record Lorenza Fisk Work." Embroidery. Waltham, Massachusetts, 1811.
Winterthur Museum, 1969.430.

Figure 85 [checklist 53]. Daniel Harrington / Anna Munroe family tree. "Lucebia Windship's Work." Embroidery, Middlesex County, Massachusetts (Lexington), circa 1812. Courtesy of the Lexington Historical Society, 12913.

Fruits of the Tree of Life

Figure 86 [checklist 69]. Jonathan Billings / Rebeckah Hapgood family tree. "Wrought by Sophia Billings aged 14." Embroidery. Middlesex County, Massachusetts (Acton), 1827. Private collection. Image courtesy of M. Finkel & Daughter.

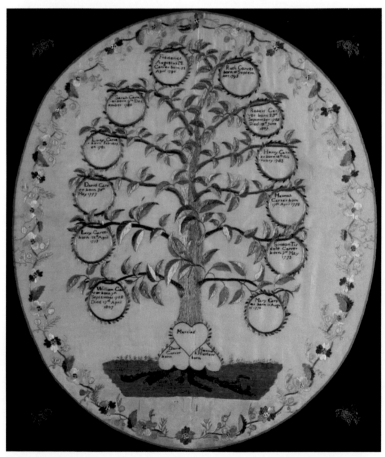

Figure 87 [checklist 74]. David Carver / Hannah Harlow family tree. Attributed to Ruth Carver. Embroidery. Taunton, Massachusetts, 1807 to 1810. Dan and Marty Campanelli, *Family Tree Samplers, 1759–1894*. Online database at *AmericanAncestors.org*, NEHGS, 2013.

Figure 88 [checklist 100]. Ebenezer Spencer / Mehetabel Buswel family tree. "Record of the family of Ebenezer Spencer of Peacham County of caledonia and State of Vermont." Watercolor. Peacham, Vermont, 1805. United States National Archive RD-DC-1.

The Spread of the Twin-Heart Motif

The concentration of the motif in Nantucket, Gloucester, and Middlesex County suggests that the twin-heart family registers were continued only during the lifetimes of the principal artists who made them or of the artist/teachers who used them in their school curriculum. Like preindustrial language or juvenile speech, the motif tended to be retentive and idiosyncratic—that is, it seemed to stay where it was and did not influence or "take over" other competing genealogical themes. But the image did occasionally seep into other neighborhoods. We can begin our understanding of this inverse dynamic by examining where the motif might predictably have spread but where in fact it failed to migrate. Despite a rich tradition of schools, teachers, calligraphers, and decorative artists, only four genealogical documents using a twin-heart design have so far surfaced either in the lower Connecticut Valley or in the upper Connecticut River Valley of Vermont and New Hampshire or even in the upper Hudson Valley. One is the Spencer/Buswel family tree (*Figure 88*) [checklist 100], drawn in 1805 in Peacham, County of Caledonia, Vermont, where two horizontally touching hearts suspend nine children tied to the parents with colored bands. This version is unrelated to the Massachusetts ones, and it employs old-fashioned "roundels" for the children, each one numbered 1st, 2nd, 3rd, and so on. There is no indication that this design ever caught on in the area. A second twin-heart example—again completely unlike the Massachusetts ones—was the 1831 Janes/Parker family record embroidered in Cornwall, Vermont, by their 11-year-old daughter [checklist 101]. The parents' birthplaces and dates are stitched at the top, as is their marriage date, 18 January 1816, which is sewn into two hearts; a long vine connects the hearts to the maker, Lucretia Janes (born 1820), with births and deaths in the family displayed on either side. A third was done in Stephentown, New York (an Albany suburb), for a family that had originally come from Rhode Island. The Jolls/Salsbury family tree (*Figure 89*) [checklist 105] names the parents on two interlocked hearts connected with ribbons of vines leading to children (in roundels) on either side. Arthur B. and Sybil B. Kern have identified the maker, Samuel Morton, as part of the William Murray Fraktur school and have suggested that the piece was possibly executed as a school exercise.[61] A fourth example is the

Wheeler/Wing, Wheeler/Goodnow register [checklist 81], a watercolor that seems to echo the Lexington or Middlesex motif but is in no way a copy of the design; it is a late piece (after 1848) and was done in Montpelier, Vermont.

This paucity of surviving examples of the emblem in a region of isolated and rural distances, constant emigration of new families, and a long-standing decorative tradition that enveloped the entire valley in the late eighteenth and early nineteenth centuries comes as a real surprise. But the twin-heart motif also failed to gain a foothold in upper New York State or in any areas well outside New England, like the Ohio River Valley, the Appalachian foothills, or the middle and southern states. The symbol also failed to gain acceptance in the Fraktur traditions followed in Philadelphia and rural Pennsylvania despite their prominent use of heart emblems. Why were these regions unresponsive to this vernacular influence? Was the motif deemed by successful farming or trading families or by teachers of female academies as being too familiar? Was it viewed as childish? The answer eludes us, but a clue might be found in the noticeable hesitance of most New Englanders to travel beyond the circle of towns in their immediate neighborhood, which produced an insularity that characterized the region during the transitioning decades we are talking about.

When the twin-heart motif did move, distances usually remained small. The motif circulated internally along the Massachusetts and Connecticut coastlines for intervals of about 10 or 20 miles; it reached adjoining portions of New Hampshire and coastal Maine following established packet routes of 30 to 40 miles. These distances are almost lost in a colonial or early American setting, and it took place outside the newspaper- or handbill-based advertising that accompanied major shifts in early American fashion or taste. By contrast, the "physiognotrace" (which made cheap miniatures and profiles), electrical remedies, automatons, and even shifts in wearing apparel (such as the Suwarrow boot) all moved throughout the United States with lightning speed, and shopkeepers and merchants typically grounded their spread to prior contacts in an Atlantic world based in London, Edinburgh, Dublin, or Paris.[62]

Transfers of the motif took place in two ways. First, some schools occasionally drew pupils from well outside their own community. When Samuel Rodman, an enterprising and successful Newport-born Quaker married Elizabeth Rotch in 1780, the union was celebrated in Sherborn, a small community on Nantucket where Elizabeth was born in 1757. The family had nine children on the island between 1781 and 1794. As Samuel Rodman's candle business prospered, however, the couple built a large home 50 miles away in New Bedford in 1798 to raise their family. Nevertheless, their youngest daughter, Sarah Rodman (born 1793), who is thought to have been the artist, may have gone to school in Nantucket and maintained her contacts, selecting an island style design (*Figure 42*) [checklist 10] when she painted a watercolor family tree for her father and mother.[63] This

Figure 89 [checklist 105]. Jeremiah Jolls / Roby Salsbury family tree. Signed: "Drawn by S. Morton." Watercolor. Stephentown (Albany), New York, 1806–1815. Winterthur Museum, 1960.324.

piece gives the initial impression of being a "Nantucket" family tree design that left the island, but it was probably occasioned instead by her own and her mother's birthplace there.

In other instances, these types of transfers may have taken place more directly through the movement of home-trained artists following the flow of family ties. Because colors and paper were now readily accessible to Massachusetts and New Hampshire households, a number of what seem to be watercolor imitations of the basic Lexington or Middlesex County embroidered version of the motif appear. These look-alikes, which are still being found, surface in western portions of Middlesex County and adjoining areas of Worcester County and southern New Hampshire. Each one tells a different story, but at least three of them suggest the existence of a larger patterning among the Stearns (or Sterns) and Davis families of Middlesex and Worcester Counties as well as the possible role of a local schoolteacher or mentor who may have taught the concept to his pupils.

We begin with a document that has ties to Billerica, a town that borders Bedford and Carlisle. The image shows a tree celebrating the 1800 marriage of John Sterns and Mary Lane and the birth of their eight children between 1802 and 1815 (Sterns/Lane, *Figure 90*) [checklist 76]. The shape of the tree and the associated decorative work indicate that the unidentified watercolorist was familiar with the basic embroidered emblem, perhaps through examples like Davis/Stearns (*Figure 91*) [checklist 45], or another like it, and painted one to match it. Noticeable on Sterns/Lane are the multicolored striped fronds or branches holding up each side of the paired hearts, a key element of the Lexington design. Similar fronds are found on eight of the embroidered pieces, but only one of these is striped. A parent in the Sterns/Lane piece, John Stearns (1765–1836) of Billerica, son of Hon. Isaac and Sarah Abbott Stearns, was the younger brother of Sarah Stearns (1759–1807),

a parent in the Davis/Stearns piece. Each sibling had children whose births were celebrated with twin-heart records—in other words, a possible sharing of taste among siblings and cousins. According to the genealogist Avis Stearns Van Wagenen, John Stearns is known to have owned a picture with heart-shaped devices prominently displayed in his Billerica house-hold.[64] This may have been the Sterns/Lane watercolor cited above or possibly a now-lost Sterns/Lane embroidery from which it may have been copied. In either event, the result may have been a fairly exact watercolor replication of the design.[65]

Figure 90 [checklist 76]. John Sterns / Mary Lane family tree. Watercolor. Middlesex County, Massachusetts (Billerica), circa 1816–1820. Former collection of Edith G. Halpert. Location unknown.

Figure 91 [checklist 45]. Thaddeus Davis / Sarah Stearns family tree. Embroidery. Stitched marriage date not correct. Middlesex County (Bedford or Billerica), circa 1800. Location unknown. Photograph provided by Sandy Macfarlane.

Figure 92 [checklist 78]. Josiah Davis / Abigail Hubbard family tree. Watercolor. Concord, Massachusetts, or New Ipswich, New Hampshire, circa 1810–1816. Before restoration. Courtesy of Alderfer Auction.

Figure 93 [checklist 78]. Josiah Davis / Abigail Hubbard family tree. Concord, Massachusetts, or New Ipswich, New Hampshire, circa 1810–1816. After restoration. Location unknown.

Fruits of the Tree of Life

This represents one case where a Davis/Stearns relationship may have led to the transfer of the concept. A second document in turn leads us to New Ipswich, New Hampshire, a town located just north of the New Hampshire border. A watercolor design similar in some ways to the Sterns/Lane piece, it appears to follow the movement of a Concord, Massachusetts, family to New Ipswich in 1773, the year when Josiah Davis took his new wife Abigail Hubbard and his 1-year-old son Josiah to start his life as a farmer and cotton mill owner there. The Davis/Hubbard tree (*Figures 92 and 93*) [checklist 78], presumably done sometime after 1810, shows the birth of thirteen more children that included one set of twins (Cyrus and Cyrene, born 15 February 1800). Like the Sterns/Lane piece, it has most of the design elements of the embroidered group including the multicolored striped fronds holding the parental hearts together (although the shape of the tree is different). Especially noticeable are the twins side by side on one limb, and the yellow versus brown gender coloration of the apples. Severed stems accompanied by flag-like inscriptions note the deaths of four of the children.[66]

The scene now turns to Ashburnham, a Massachusetts town located on the other side of Fitchburg and just south of New Ipswich. Two of Hon. Isaac and Sarah Abbott Stearns's other sons, Isaac (born 1750) and William (born 1752), moved to Ashburnham to become farmers; and their parents Isaac and Sarah, who still resided in Billerica, were accustomed to visit them even as an elderly couple who "rode to Ashburnham in one day."[67] The Stearnses' tie to New Ipswich becomes closer when one of the Davis/Hubbard children (Lucinda Davis) married Jesse Stearns, a teacher, surveyor, and conveyancer who was born in Ashburnham in 1784 to Isaac Stearns Jr. and Mary Crosby. In other words, Lucinda married the nephew of John Stearns, the father in the Sterns/Lane piece.

A third look-alike further cements this relationship and suggests a possible mentor. The Brooks/Winchester watercolor (*Figures 94 and 95*) [checklist 77] appears to be a schoolboy piece signed by William Brooks (approximately 13 years old), who grew up in an Ashburnham family whose father had moved there about 1782 from Lincoln. William records the birth of four siblings (three boys, one girl) and an unnamed stillborn. The piece is carefully but painfully made, the artist attempting to follow dotted lines apparently marked out in advance. He employs the usual visual conventions (no stem on the stillborn apple, different colors for boys and girls), and he signs it with his name written in large letters. The piece suggests the possibility that "Master Jesse" Stearns of Ashburnham, who served the town as a well-known schoolteacher for over twenty years, taught the concept to his Ashburnham pupils and may have even brought it to New Ipswich when he moved there with Lucinda in 1820.[68]

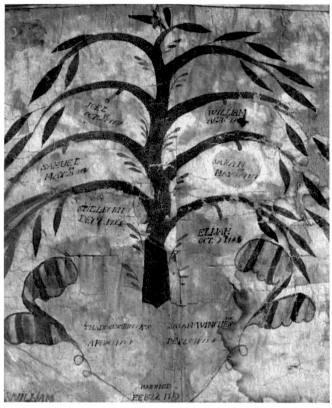

Figure 94 [checklist 77]. Thaddeus Brooks / Sarah Winchester family register. Signed: "William Brooks" (born 1803). Watercolor. Ashburnham, Massachusetts, circa 1814. Location unknown. Sold on eBay, March 2019, by Katesy7777, item 352614394227.

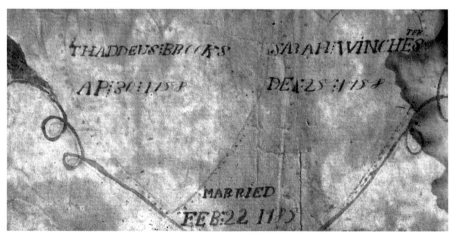

Figure 95 [checklist 77]. Detail. Thaddeus Brooks / Sarah Winchester, circa 1814.

Fruits of the Tree of Life

At least two more examples are known in this look-alike series. The Clement/ Pierce family tree (*Figure 96*) [checklist 79] celebrates the 1805 Townsend marriage between John Clement and Hannah Pierce and lists their eight children born between 1805 and 1824. Like the others, the piece shares key characteristics with the Middlesex County–area embroidered group, including its use of looping, multicolored fronds supporting the hearts—although the tree shape is different from the embroidered ones. However, it closely resembles an embroidery by Mary Russell (*Figure 75*) [checklist 55] with the same coronation of white flowers. In this case, no family ties are there to help us. Hannah Pierce was born in Townsend, and John Clement was born in Dracut, where as a young man he worked as a carpenter.[69] The Clement/Pierce tree might be an imitation of a stitched genealogy or it could be simply school-taught, but it does support the notion that western portions of Middlesex County and towns like New Ipswich and Sharon served as a rallying point for watercolor genealogical art done in this pattern.

The final watercolor look-alike comes a few years later, and again the maker is known. The Eleazer Davis/Martha Skinner tree (*Figure 97*) [checklist 80], signed by Hannah S. Davis in 1826, represents a family residing in Bedford, a Middlesex town close to the likely point of origin of the embroidered symbol that it copied. Possibly tied in some way to the Davis families of New Ipswich, Ashburnham, or Bedford, the document is unusual because it celebrates the marriage of the parents with a pair of blue birds standing or fluttering over the hearts—a characteristic not shared by the Middlesex group. It does preserve other conventions of the embroideries, however, such as the back-and-forth undulation of the tree; the differentiation between white and reddish apples; the intersection of the two hearts; and the marriage date posted between the hearts. That it is a later copy is not only indicated by its date, but by the decorative stenciling on the horizontal ground line the tree stands on. Hannah was only 13 at the time, and it seems to be an exercise in watercolor draftsmanship and calligraphy.

The real question posed by these look-alike documents involves eastern Massachusetts and southern New Hampshire geography. Why did the image drift inland into recently incorporated and isolated rural towns only a short distance (about a day's ride westward) from their sources and not northward into northern New Hampshire and the Connecticut Valley and beyond? We can only speculate an answer. The most likely explanation is that these locations provided farms for families emigrating from the immediate Middlesex communities, but they were still relatively close by. Households that owned and enjoyed these embroidered pieces may have asked their relatives or neighborhood amateur artists to make ones like them in watercolor. In other words, when residents of Middlesex County towns (among them Bedford, Lexington, Billerica, and Concord) moved further inland into western Middlesex County and northern Worcester County towns (Fitchburg,

Lunenburg, Townsend, Ashburnham, and Ashby), they took more than their furniture and household goods; they literally took their tastes and expectations with them. If they relocated further into southern New Hampshire—for example, into Sharon and New Ipswich in Hillsborough County, and Marlborough in Cheshire County—they did the same thing as long as they were still close to their hometowns. Some may even have sent their children to Middlesex County schools, all while keeping in touch with relatives and contacts in their town of origin. For example, while Lucy Hubbard Rice [checklist 72] was born and raised in Ashby, Massachusetts, her mother was born in nearby Concord in 1775. Both Lucy's embroidery and that of her younger sister Elmira Rice [checklist 73] (now unlocated) show indications of the Middlesex–area genealogical hearts–and–tree style. If these samplers were school-taught pieces (as they most likely were), it is probably fair to assume that the mother chose a school in the eastern Middlesex area with which she was familiar to send her daughters as boarders. Or, if they were simply household exercises, that she asked them to follow a pattern or copybook she brought with her to Ashby in which the genealogical design was articulated. By contrast, if they moved further into central New Hampshire and Vermont and parts of upper New York state, families were likely to lose contact with such design sources and not keep up this localized and idiosyncratic tradition.

During this same period, however, at least two new genealogical watercolorists had become active in New England, and both drew to some extent on the Middlesex County motif. One, unidentified, found clients in the immediate Fitchburg, Townsend, Ashby, and Sharon areas in western Middlesex County; a second, known only by initials, ranged from Boston up through the Maine coastline. Both artists were probably semiprofessional practitioners. The first was responsible for three twin-heart family registers and a half-completed twin-heart sample design and seems to have been working initially in and around Fitchburg, a town just south of Townsend. A watercolor painted by this artist for the 1796 marriage of Asa Farwell and Vashti Carter of Fitchburg (*Figure 98*) [checklist 82] employs a poplar-filled landscape with six children named on a large central apple tree. It is a quiet design, punctuated by the ribbon that ties together the two hearts at the base of the tree. A two-story federal-style home stands to the right. A second watercolor by this artist, celebrating the 1808 marriage of Adde Jaquith and Abigail Whiting of Ashby (*Figure 99*) [checklist 83] and done about 1823, also generally follows the Middlesex County embroidered format, but does not attempt to copy it. The hearts, which seem proportionally larger, are set in a landscape of modest houses, fields, and poplar trees; each child is given a limb, grey apples for girls, orange apples for boys. Two houses and what appears to be a meetinghouse, or perhaps a windmill, provide an architectural background. A third in this same genre was made for Polly or Patty Wyman and Samuel Ryan (*Figure 100*) [checklist 84], who lived in Sharon and New Ipswich, New Hampshire, just over the border from Ashby. She married twice, producing children in each union. Known now only from an auctioneer's image, the watercolor Sawyer/Wyman, Ryan/Wyman register shows an apple tree rising from three hearts, with meandering flowers on either side.

All three of these family trees exhibit new visual protocols and indicate the parents' marriage and the deaths of the children before adulthood. The lover's knot on the Farwell/Carter piece may be the first time we encounter this visual conceit in New England's family-tree iconography. Found on signet rings, mourning jewelry, earrings, bracelets, broaches, and valentines in the eighteenth and early nineteenth centuries, this icon was characteristically a sign of "having tied the knot"; but there is no evidence that its use on family trees started in central Massachusetts, and it may have been copied from another source. Elsewhere, on the Sawyer/Wyman, Ryan/Wyman register, Patty is represented as one of three hearts clustered at the base of the tree; the upper two list the names of her first and second husbands. On the Jaquith piece, death notices are stylized and incorporated into the design, each child bearing a prominent blank husk on the same branch as the apple. None of these variations is seen in the earlier Gloucester or Middlesex County pieces.

The second watercolorist, who appears to have had some kind of contact with the first, demonstrates some of these same visual characteristics including the ribbons that tie the hearts together. Equally important, he or she introduces Nantucket characteristics seldom seen on the mainland. The New England Historic Genealogical Society, which owns two of the four family trees attributed to this individual, identifies this artist as "J. P." because these initials appear in the lower right corner of both pieces.[70] Evidence of this artist comes initially from a tree made for the 1770 marriage of Josiah Jones and Susannah Bennett and their children (*Figure 101*) [checklist 87]. The Joneses lived in Lunenburg, a town that adjoins Fitchburg, Ashby, and Townsend, and the piece dates to sometime after 1796 when most of the children were adults. The artist presumably interacted with the unidentified Fitchburg/Townsend calligrapher because both share the same ribbon binding the hearts found on the Farwell/Carter family tree. Other J. P. characteristics include the wording of the label, the prominent spacing for death notices, and the manner of placing the deaths of the parents just under the hearts. Only the rose-like intertwining of the tree limbs is different and represents what may be the fourth time that this seemingly "Nantucket" style had actually left the island. About a decade later a more mature J. P. seems to be living in Boston where he or she made the tree for Caleb Coolidge and Rebecca Edwards (*Figures 102 and 103*) [checklist 88]; this document has a pronounced Boston connection since the Coolidges were married in that city in 1784 and later lived there and possibly in Charlestown. Nevertheless, some of their children were born in Machias, Maine, and it is possible the piece was done in that community.

The two later J. P. pieces, however, definitely appear to be based in coastal Maine. The family register for Amos Pearson and Marcy Sevey (*Figures 104 and 105*) [checklist 90] indicates they were married in Pownalborough, in 1772, and had seven children between 1773 and 1784, the youngest being Betsy who as an adult married a James Patterson of nearby Dresden, possibly the "J. P." cited on the document. A second family register was made for Samuel Matthews and Abigail Chessley (*Figures 106 and 107*) [checklist 89], who were married in 1762 in "Georgies," Maine, perhaps the town of Castine, since that is the birthplace of their daughter Miriam, born in 1763, and of their son Samuel Matthews Jr., born in 1766. But at least one parent retained a Boston connection: Abigail Chessley Matthews, "formerly of Castine," died in Boston in 1811.[71]

Despite their geographical spread, J. P.'s watercolors reflect a consistent pattern of symbolism and seem to be aimed (like others in the Fitchburg/Townsend group) at unborn readers. All three embed the hearts in a rural or wooded landscape. Each child is marked by an apple tied to an individual branch. Each one provides unattached, colorless apple husks to mark the deaths of the children; two of the three provide colorless hearts to mark the deaths of parents. Each document is appropriately titled "A Record of the Births and Deaths" of its respective family, in effect providing what amounted to a paper document to be filled out later at the appropriate time. Still unexplained, however, is the similarity of the binding ribbon between the Farwell/Carter piece and those on the three J. P. pieces. Not only are individual folds, curves, and twists of the ribbon similar on all four pieces, but the language, typography, dates, and marriage sites follow the same style or close to the same. And why did the calligrapher use a ribbon? Was it part of a premarital "handfasting" ceremony in which the couple physically tied themselves together with a ribbon or rope, a custom still practiced in some English-speaking cultures to this day? Handfasting was seen in medieval Scotland as a trial marriage, part of an old Celtic protocol that proved the worthiness of the union before it was validated by children. The reappearance of a binding emblem as a symbol of marriage on an early nineteenth-century New England genealogy may mean little more than a couple "tying the knot," but it may also suggest some form of carryover from centuries-old past practices.[72]

Fruits of the Tree of Life

Figure 96 [checklist 79]. John Clement / Hannah Pierce family tree. Watercolor. Townsend, Massachusetts, circa 1825. Collection of Rita King.

Figure 97 [checklist 80]. Eleazer Davis / Martha Skinner family tree. "Hannah S. Davis. Bedford [Massachusetts] 1826." Watercolor. Photograph courtesy of Skinner, Inc., www.skinnerinc.com.

Figure 98 [checklist 82]. Asa Farwell / Vashti Carter family tree. Watercolor. Fitchburg, Massachusetts, circa 1810. Ex collection Pam Boynton. Photograph courtesy of Skinner, Inc., www.skinnerinc.com.

Fruits of the Tree of Life

Figure 99 [checklist 83]. Adde Jaquith / Abigail Whiting family tree. Watercolor. Ashby, Massachusetts, or New Ipswich, New Hampshire, circa 1823.

Figure 100 [checklist 84]. Family tree for the marriages of Josiah Sawyer / Patty Wyman and Samuel Ryan / Patty Wyman Sawyer. Watercolor. Sharon or New Ipswich, New Hampshire, circa 1825. Location unknown. Photograph taken from Sotheby Parke Bernet, *Important Frakturs* (1974).

Figure 101 [checklist 87]. Josiah Jones / Susannah Bennett family tree. Watercolor. Lunenburg, Massachusetts, after 1796. Susannah's last child came from her second marriage to Samuel Lawrence. Location unknown.

Figure 102 [checklist 88]. Caleb Coolidge / Rebecca Edwards family tree.
Attributed to J. P. Watercolor. Boston, Massachusetts, or Machias, Maine,
circa 1815–1825. Location unknown. Ex collection Mr. and Mrs. Jerome W. Blum.

Figure 103 [checklist 88]. Detail. Caleb Coolidge / Rebecca Edwards family tree. Boston, Massachusetts, or Machias, Maine.

Figure 104 [checklist 90]. Amos Pearson / Marcy Sevey family register. Signed: "J. P."
Watercolor. Pownalborough, Maine, circa 1815–1820. NEHGS, R. Stanton Avery Special
Collections, Mss 1075.

Fruits of the Tree of Life

Figure 105 [checklist 90]. Detail. Amos Pearson / Marcy Sevey family register.

Figure 106 [checklist 89]. Samuel Matthews / Abigail Chessley family tree.
Signed: "J. P." Watercolor. Georgies (Castine?), Maine, circa 1815–1825.
NEHGS, R. Stanton Avery Special Collections, Mss 1078.

Fruits of the Tree of Life

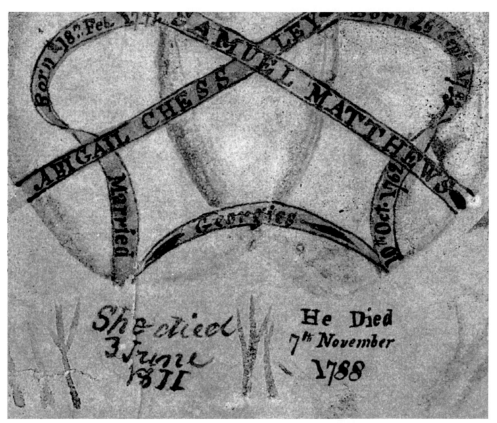

Figure 107 [checklist 89]. Detail. Samuel Matthews / Abigail Chessley family register.

Figure 108 [checklist 91]. Enoch Blake / Lydia Smith family tree.
Attributed to Joseph Odiorne. Watercolor. Pittsfield, New Hampshire,
circa 1823. Location unknown. Photograph courtesy of Donald R. Randall.

Figure 109. Certificate of intention between Enoch Blake Jr.
and Miss Lydia Smith, both of Pittsfield, New Hampshire.
Signed: "Joseph Odiorne {T. Clerk." Ink on paper.
Photograph courtesy of Donald R. Randall.

Other Examples of Artistic Transfer

In some instances, the movement of the twin-heart design may have been brought about by marriages in which one partner came from well outside the immediate area of where the calligraphist was operating. The Fifth Parish in Gloucester was so insular that Saville's and Pool's designs almost never left that community. In fact, only one example of the eighteen in that series identifies a parent located beyond Gloucester's immediate town limits. Andrew Bickford, a farmer and laborer, was "Born [in 1783] in Gilmantown," a town in Belknap County, central New Hampshire. Bickford married Olive Clark, "Born [in 1790] in Gloucester." This marriage took place in 1808 and was later documented (about 1828) by Joshua Pool Jr. [checklist 38] in a design that ostensibly depicts the Gloucester farmyard where their eight children grew up. There is no evidence that Andrew Bickford ever returned to New Hampshire, and birth records indicate that all their children were born in Gloucester, including the last three, Lucy, William, and William, who are entered on the Bickford/Clark record with handwriting different from that of Joshua Pool; both Andrew and Olive died in Gloucester.[73]

Nevertheless, some sort of tie to central New Hampshire may have been precipitated by Bickford's origin there. Pool's twin-heart motif seems to have provided the rationale (though definitely not the model) for several formal family trees attributed to Joseph Odiorne, a schoolteacher and town clerk in Pittsfield, New Hampshire[74] (located immediately south of Gilmanton), who had studied calligraphy and had some affinity for design. Odiorne appears to have echoed a Saville or Pool piece when he created the Enoch Blake/Lydia Smith family register (*Figure 108*) [checklist 91] around 1823.[75] This watercolor shows a tree growing out of three overlapping hearts sitting on a small earth mound and names two children, Elizabeth M. Blake (born 1823) and Hannah E. Blake (born 1820). These appear to be written in a different hand, suggesting Odiorne did not wait until the birth of the children before passing the document to the parents. The presence of an announcing angel in the tree as well as details of both the apples and the foliage indicate the artist did not duplicate any previous Gloucester or Nantucket models. The document's sale to the dealer Donald R. Randall was accompanied by a finely drawn certificate of marriage intention between Enoch and Lydia signed by "Joseph Odiorne {T. Clerk" of Pittsfield, 25 July 1818 (*Figure 109*), which may serve to identify him.

Figure 110 [checklist 93]. Jonathan Connor / Mary Allen family tree. Watercolor. 15 x 12 in. Gilmanton Ironworks, New Hampshire, circa 1810–1820. Former collection of Arthur B. and Sybil B. Kern. Image courtesy of Skinner, Inc., www.skinnerinc.com.

A second piece attributed to Odiorne, the Connor/Allen family tree (*Figure 110*) [checklist 93], celebrates the union and eleven children of Jonathan Connor and his wife Mary Allen who were married in 1787 in Gilmanton Ironworks, New Hampshire, so-called from an unprofitable iron smelting company started in that portion of the town in the early nineteenth century. (Connor was a grandson of one of the eighteenth-century proprietors of Gilmanton.)[76] Recently offered on the market by the estate of Arthur B. and Sybil B. Kern, the register is much more colorful (although more crudely made) than the Blake/Smith tree. But it shares the same attenuated flower sprigs, the same announcing angel and motto, and the same filled-in areas where the three hearts overlap. One other Odiorne-related register has a Gilmanton tie. This is suggested by what may be a partial copy of an Odiorne drawing that memorialized the descendants of Benjamin Sleeper and Miriam Clough (*Figure 111*) [checklist 95], both born in Gilmanton, New Hampshire, in 1779. This document has much in common with the Connor/Allen piece. But it is entirely possible that this register, which records the death of their grandson Edwin A. Kelley, who perished in the Civil War battle at Chancellorsville in 1863, was made in the 1860s and is an imitation of what is presumed to be a missing Odiorne family record; owners of this document continued to annotate it into the twentieth century.

Fruits of the Tree of Life

Figure 111 [checklist 95]. Benjamin Sleeper / Miriam Clough "A family record."
Family of Samuel G. Kelley and Amanda A. Sleeper and marriage of Melvin
W. Young and Ellen G. Kelley shown above. Watercolor. Gilmanton, New
Hampshire, circa 1863–1865? Courtesy of Historic New England. Gift of
Constance McCann Betts, Helena Woolworth Guest and Frasier W. McCann,
1942.2342.1AB.

Curiously, an Odiorne-type image is also known to have made its way back to Massachusetts. A family register made for the 1774 marriage of the Newbury chair-maker Joseph Davis and Hannah Akus (*Figure 112*) [checklist 94] has most of the Odiorne characteristics, especially the clustered three-part heart arrangement. But in this instance, it is signed by William Hodges, presumably a grandchild, and it seems to have been a school exercise. The only good reason a Newbury-born child would come up with a New Hampshire genealogical image of his grandfather's family would be because there was a family connection between Newbury and south-central New Hampshire. Not surprisingly, Hannah Akus or Akers, daughter of Moses and Abigail Daniels, was born in South Hampton, Rockingham County, New Hampshire.[77]

Once established in Belknap County, however, the twin-heart image may have persisted there. Sometime in the early nineteenth century, a member of the Seavey family of Chichester, New Hampshire (a community which adjoins Pittsfield to the south), memorialized the 1796 marriage and seven children (born between 1797 and 1811) of George Seavey and Betsey Lane in an original but crudely drawn watercolor tree of life (*Figure 113*) [checklist 96] attached to two prone intersecting hearts. When their youngest girl, Betsey Lane Seavey, married Col. James Drake in 1834, the bride carried this document with her to her new household, and it was sold as part of the Drake estate in Pittsfield in 1987.[78]

Occasionally, too, twin-heart family trees were made by calligraphers for personal or private reasons. John B. Copp, a home-schooled deaf artist from Stonington, Connecticut, had learned to copy others' calligraphy and artwork, and he likely had access to a family register that closely resembled the Folger/Starbuck [checklist 3] and Folger/Folger [checklist 13] pieces both in its style and substance. According to Brian S. Ehrlich's study of this artist,[79] Copp inserted his own family's genealogy into a Nantucket design, citing himself as one of the children: "John Brown [Copp] born 2d August 1779." The resulting Deacon Samuel Copp/Dolley Brown family tree (*Figure 41*) [checklist 4] looks like a transmission of the motif out of Nantucket, but it seems likely to be a single example by a copyist who had temporary use of an original. It is possible Copp created the piece sometime between 1810 and 1815 while on a visit to that island where he came in contact with the Folger household.[80]

Genealogically oriented hearts were also generated by (or taught to) school children. The Joseph Camp / Anna Kellogg watercolor (*Figure 114*) [checklist 104] was drawn in 1787 by 14-year-old Anna Camp in Newington, Connecticut, a small farming village that once was part of Wethersfield. Anna's design consists of a brilliant medley of hearts within hearts, doubled and tripled hearts, all set off with a single black coffin. No doubt part of her upbringing as a member of a

Figure 112 [checklist 94]. Detail. Joseph Davis Jr. / Hannah Akus family tree. "Drawn by William Hodges." Watercolor. Newburyport, Massachusetts, or South Hampton, New Hampshire, circa 1800. Sold by Garth's Auctioneers and Appraisers in 2013.

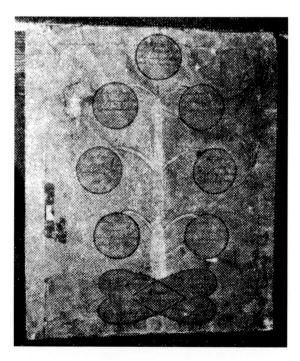

Figure 113 [checklist 96]. George Seavey / Betsey Lane family tree. Watercolor. Chichester, New Hampshire, after 1811.

larger community aware of its dedication to literacy and to genealogical outreach, the document underscores the emotional underpinnings of rural life and reveals how eighteenth-century families saw themselves as a single unit. Elsewhere, school children in Newbury, Massachusetts, drew heart-related family registers to learn calligraphy and drawing in much the same way. In 1807 13-year-old Harriet Perkins composed a "Genealogi[c]al Family Piece" featuring two hearts and compass-made roundels for her parents Benjamin Perkins and Dorcas Stanwood [checklist 106]. A much younger schoolmate and possibly a relative named Atkinson Stanwood followed the same pattern when he composed the first of two genealogies of Joseph Stanwood's family (*Figure 115*) [checklist 109] that placed nine children—each one provided with a birth date—within the confines of its own half circle. In the second (*Figure 116*) [checklist 110], made in 1816, he placed the names inside a large heart. Near the top of each document are half-circles depicting his father, his father's first wife, his mother, and his stepmother. Atkinson did not name the school or teacher where he drew these records, but another pupil at this school did. Daniel Moody Lankester drew two genealogies for his grandfather Daniel Dodge, both done in 1809, using compass-made roundels and a large heart to hold the family together. The November 4 image (*Figure 117*) [checklist 107] reflected his grandfather's first marriage to Martha Moody; the November 13 record (*Figures 118 and 119*) [checklist 108] included Daniel's second wife Mary Kimball while also naming his school and teacher: "Newbury East-School / B. H. Cheever." Little is known of Benjamin Hale Cheever (1770–1822). Born in Newbury, one of three brothers, he was married to Rebeckah Tompson (died 1832) in Newbury in 1795 and was identified as a trustee of the Newburyport Sabbath School and Tract Society in 1820. There were few Cheevers in this part of eastern Massachusetts. Benjamin may have been a descendant of Ezekiel Cheever of Ipswich and Boston who died in 1708 and had a long-standing reputation as hating periwigs.[81]

Finally, some amateur calligraphers ignored regional or school-taught motifs and created their own designs. The most striking example is the Cheever/Eustes family tree (*Figure 120*) [checklist 97], which celebrates the 1765 marriage of Joshua Cheever and Abigail Eustes of Chelsea, Massachusetts. This piece is signed by Edward Pratt of Chelsea and dated 30 December 1799. Pratt's image depicts two hearts nourishing a pear tree festooned with nine yellow and red ripened fruits representing children and two yellowed pears hanging on whitened and withered limbs specifying children who had died. Miscellaneous husbandry and farming equipment (yoke, rake, shovel, scythe) is shown on either side of the hearts. This is the only known pear tree using the twin-heart concept, but there may have been imitators of that motif in the Chelsea neighborhood. It might also be argued that the tree's trunk looks like a cannon: Joshua's father Nathan Cheever was a member of the Ancient and Honorable Artillery Company in Boston.[82] Another self-taught model, the Joshua Foss and Elizabeth Hunt genealogy (*Figure 121*) [checklist 99] with ties to Rye, New Hampshire, employs circles rather than hearts to identify both parents and children in what may have been a poorly drawn imitation of another more polished image. Few, if any, of these twin-heart or heart-within-heart variants are associated with any school or known teachers or calligraphers; they reveal no direct or stylistic links to any of the other registers and are unrelated to any movement of people or the impulse to copy. They also show that the emblems of genealogical protocols—such as depicting deceased children as withered flowers, the expectation that widows of men lost at sea would remarry, or the acceptance into the family of stepchildren acquired by second and third marriages—were critical to addressing the complexities of everyday family life in the late eighteenth- and early nineteenth-century Atlantic world.

Figure 114 [checklist 104]. Joseph Camp / Anna Kellogg family tree. Signed: "Made by Anna Camp in January AD 1787 &C." Watercolor. Newington, Connecticut, 1787. Copyright Newington Historical Society and Trust, Inc. Gift of the Camp Family, 79-12:55.

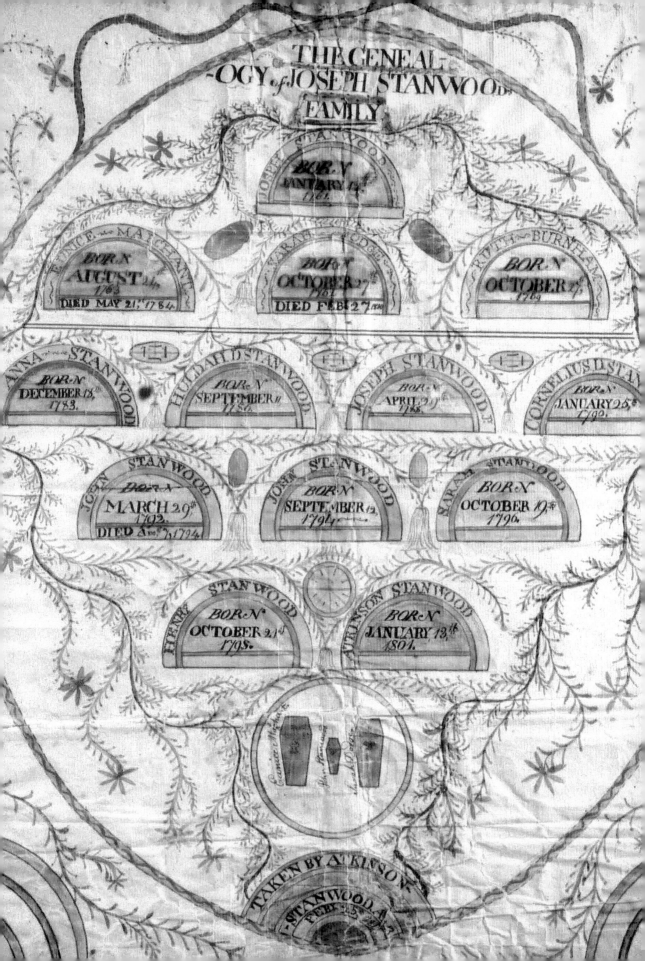

THE GENEAL- -OGY of JOSEPH STANWOOD FAMILY

JOSEPH STANWOOD BORN JANUARY 14 1761

EUNICE MARCHANT BORN AUGUST 24 1763 DIED MAY 21, 1784

SARAH HODGE BORN OCTOBER 27 1767 DIED FEB. 27 1788

RUTH BURNHAM BORN OCTOBER 27 1769

ANNA STANWOOD BORN DECEMBER 18 1783

HULDAH STANWOOD BORN SEPTEMBER 11 1786

JOSEPH STANWOOD BORN APRIL 29 1788

CORNELIUS II STAN BORN JANUARY 25 1790

JOHN STANWOOD BORN MARCH 29 1792 DIED A 7 1794

JOHN STANWOOD BORN SEPTEMBER 12 1794

SARAH STANWOOD BORN OCTOBER 19 1796

HENRY STANWOOD BORN OCTOBER 21 1798

ATKINSON STANWOOD BORN JANUARY 13 1801

TAKEN BY ATKINSON STANWOOD A FEB 5

(left page) Figure 115 [checklist 109]. Joseph Stanwood / Eunice Marchant, Joseph Stanwood / Sarah Dodge, Joseph Stanwood / Ruth Burnham family tree. Signed: "Taken by Atkinson Stanwood Aet 13 / Feby 25th 1814." Attributed to the East School. Watercolor. Newbury, Massachusetts, 1814. From the Collections of the Museum of Old Newbury.

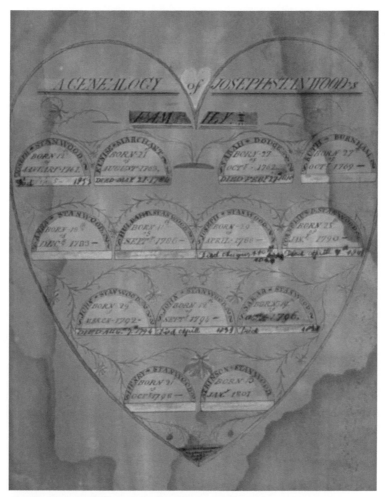

Figure 116 [checklist 110]. Joseph Stanwood / Eunice Marchant, Joseph Stanwood / Sarah Dodge, Joseph Stanwood / Ruth Burnham family tree. Signed: "Atkinson Stanwood. Newburyport, June 7 1816." Attributed to the East School. Watercolor. Newbury, Massachusetts, 1816. Courtesy of Historic New England. Gift of Bertram K. and Nina Fletcher Little, 1992.464.

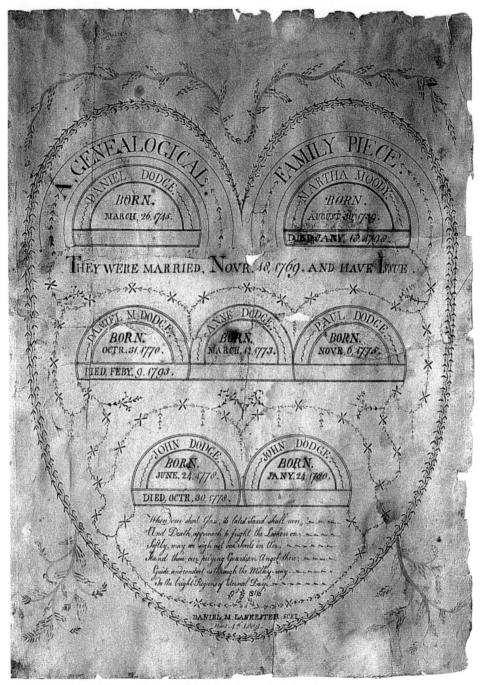

Figure 117 [checklist 107]. Daniel Dodge / Martha Moody.
"A Genealogical Family Piece." Signed: "Daniel M. Lankester Scrt. Nov 4th 1809."
Attributed to the East School. Watercolor. Newbury, Massachusetts, 1809. NEHGS.

Fruits of the Tree of Life

Figure 118 [checklist 108].
Daniel Dodge / Martha Moody /
Mary Dudley. "A Genealogical Family
Piece." Signed: "Daniel Moody Lankester.
Æ14. Scripsit Nov' 13, 1809. Newbury
East-School, B. H. Cheever." Watercolor.
Newbury, Massachusetts, 1809. NEHGS.

Figure 119 [checklist 108]. Detail. Daniel Dodge / Martha Moody / Mary Dudley.
"A Genealogical Family Piece." "Scripsit Nov' 13, 1809."

Figure 120 [checklist 97]. Joshua Cheever / Abigail Eustes family tree.
Signed: "By Edward Pratt Chelsea Decem^r 30th 1799 (No 3)." Watercolor.
Chelsea, Massachusetts, 1799. Leslie and Peter Warwick.

Fruits of the Tree of Life

Figure 121 [checklist 99]. Joshua Foss / Elizabeth Hunt family tree. Watercolor. Rye, New Hampshire, circa 1820–1840. Posted on eBay, 20 December 2016. Courtesy of Copake Auction.

Figure 122 [checklist 43]. Blank record in Tarr computation book. Watercolor. Gloucester, Massachusetts, circa 1800–1830. John McInnis, Amesbury, Massachusetts, Auctioneers.

The Role of Calligraphers and Embroidery Teachers

A key question concerns the role of the decorative artists who produced these pieces or made the design part of their curriculum. Were these semiprofessional watercolorists and schoolteachers tied to the communities where they worked, or did they move from community to community looking for employment? The answer seems to be mixed. About half of the Nantucket pieces appear to have been made at the homes of Phebe Folger, Rebecca Folger, and Eunice Gardner, all active members of the island community who did not travel and who may have operated temporary calligraphy and watercolor schools in or near their homes. Elsewhere the living patterns of both the school teacher William Saville and Joshua Pool (whose occupation is unknown) seemed integrated into a residential system that taught sea captains and navigators their trade in a major maritime and fishing center on Cape Ann. Most Gloucester men went to work as fishermen, mariners, or ship builders; their teachers remained in Gloucester because their academic livelihood was there. The probable maker of the Pittsfield/Gilmanton group, Joseph Odiorne of Pittsfield, was permanently tied to his neighborhood because his duties as a schoolteacher and town clerk required it. And some artists were simply neighbors and close relatives of their subjects. For example, Capt. Thomas Pratt, a first cousin of Edward Pratt of Chelsea who drew the pear tree on the Joshua Cheever / Abigail Eustes family record, married Anna Cheever, Joshua and Abigail's oldest daughter.[83]

Notwithstanding, other teachers or calligraphers seemed to have remained in town only when they found commissioned work—coming and going to locations at great distances from each other. Edward D. Burke—who is mentioned in Nantucket public records only once as the father of a young man who fell overboard from the HMS *Harlequin* and drowned in 1796—was probably a transient. He was a successful teacher, however, and joined the Nantucket Masons' Union Lodge, being "initiated" on 2 April 1792 and "raised" on 14 May of the same year. A history of freemasonry in Nantucket quoted those 1792 records 111 years later, citing Burke as "a schoolmaster from Ireland, Residing in this Town at present."[84] The phrase "at present" does not describe a permanent resident of the island. Indeed, by 1800

Burke may have been the Edward D. Burke who was advertising a mathematical and English language school in Baltimore, Maryland.[85] Daniel Stanton, presumed to be a young follower of Burke, was called a "school teacher" in an advertisement trying to locate him, but he, too, apparently moved about and was reported "missing" from Portsmouth, Rhode Island, in 1823.[86] Other possible wandering calligraphers include J. P., who painted registers for families in Pownalborough and Castine, Maine, which are about 150 miles apart and readily accessible to coastal shipping especially from vessels coming from Boston. But here, too, there is contrary evidence since the two families who patronized this artist (the Matthewses and the Pearsons) were marked by intermarriages. J. P. may also have worked for clients in Massachusetts Bay, specifically for Caleb Coolidge, who was apparently born in Boston or Roxbury in 1753 and whose second marriage (to Rebecca Edwards) was officiated in Boston by Rev. Joseph Eckley in 1784. At least two children (Mary E. Coolidge and Matilda D. Coolidge) died either in Boston or in Charlestown. This suggests that J. P. moved about on coastal vessels, and it is possible that this artist's travels may have taken him or her inland as far as Townsend and Ashby—accounting for the similarity of their painted ribbons. The unidentified calligrapher who made the Pinkham/Berry piece (who may well have been a member of the Pinkham family) apparently had enough travel experience to put him or her in contact with another artist who used the same design 250 miles away in Webster Plantation, Maine.

If calligraphers were obliged to move around constantly to maintain their trade, this may explain why solicitation for new work was so important to their careers. Among the 114 examples of the twin-heart or heart-within-heart images listed here, at least three and possibly four were blank or unfinished records that probably served as calligraphers' samples. One is the unfilled family tree (*Figure 122*) [checklist 43] that appears in a computational notebook kept by a Tarr family member in Gloucester, presumably made by a student attending Saville's school circa 1800–1830.[87] This notebook, said at one time to be housed at the Sandy Bay Historical Society in Rockport, was being sold at an auction in Amesbury in 1996.[88] The image is unmarked, but it was signed with an armorial head (resembling a devil) drawn at the tree's root. Another is an unfinished register by the unidentified Fitchburg/Townsend watercolorist known only from a photograph. This item is referenced by the parents' incomplete names "John K." and "Olive K." (*Figure 123*) [checklist 85]; the children are recorded by first names only without any dates. The tree is depicted growing in an urn blazoned with two hearts. The third is the Asa K / Sally Blake, "We Ware Marrid" family tree (*Figure 124*) [checklist 92], attributed to Joseph Odiorne, where no children are listed, an item collected by the author and dealer Peter H. Tillou in the 1970s. Tillou identified it as a New Hampshire piece, and we have tentatively attributed it to Joseph Odiorne. A fourth may have been the Thomas Sylvester / Polly Lane document (*Figure 125*) [checklist 42], which was incompletely filled out and folded over many times and may have been used by Saville as a model. If all in fact were samples, they no doubt helped calligraphers to set up temporary schools or allowed them to sell commissioned pieces. The concept of calligraphers as itinerants may help explain why J. P., whose work has stylistic ties to the Townsend/Ashby group, was willing to accommodate his or her design when serving a new group of patrons in Maine. Possibly active in two or three different places, the watercolorist may have presented a new phase to attract commissions.

The case of the Middlesex County embroidery style, however, presents a more difficult problem. While the identity of the teacher or teachers is currently unavailable, a plurality of stitchers' names (ten out of twenty-six) are associated with Lexington families. This has always led owners, collectors, textile scholars, dealers, and curators to locate the school in that particular Massachusetts town. This supposition might be entirely correct. Yet the newspaper record shows that no academies for young women were advertised in Lexington before 1822,[89] whereas some were publicized in surrounding and nearby towns, including Bedford, Burlington, Medford, Waltham, Watertown, and Woburn. Current research suggests that the most likely school location was in Bedford's town center on the road leading to Burlington. In 1797 Rev. Samuel Stearns, a Harvard graduate who was then Bedford's minister, founded a "female seminary" in the town, which attracted pupils from Bedford "and neighboring towns."[90] The school apparently thrived. In May 1806 Elijah Stearns, Samuel Stearns's first cousin, advertised in Boston's *Columbian Centinel* a "School in Bedford, near the Meeting-House" under the leadership of "Miss Sprague, ... for the instruction of young ladies in Reading, Writing, Arithmetic, Geography, English Grammar, Orthography, Composition, Painting and Embroidery."[91] Miss Sprague was probably Phebe Sprague (1784–1843), the eldest daughter of Lt. John Sprague of Bedford. Aged 22 years in 1806, Phebe remained single until about age 50 when she married her cousin William Fitch and moved to Maine.[92] Elijah Stearns, a storekeeper who later became Bedford's first postmaster, noted in the same advertisement that four young ladies could be "handsomely" accommodated at the school as boarders.[93] The links of this school to the families named in the registers are also relatively direct. Elijah Stearns was a first cousin to John Stearns of Billerica, the husband in the Sterns/Lane watercolor piece [checklist 76], and to John's sister Sarah Stearns, the wife in the Davis/Stearns embroidery [checklist 45].[94]

There are many other candidates, however. In Woburn, Joanna Haskell and Sarah Burges taught embroidery during that period. Mrs. Peabody taught embroidery in Billerica. And Susanna Rowson maintained a school for years in Medford; she was followed there by Mrs. Ann Stuart Newton (Gilbert Stuart's sister), Miss Ann Rose of London, and Miss Hannah Swan of Medford. Other candidates include Miss

Woodbridge, who taught at her brother William Woodbridge's school in Medford in 1792; Mrs. Battelle, who taught at the same school in 1795; and Bathsheba Whitman (1777–1864), born in Bridgewater, Massachusetts, who died in Lexington "after being engaged as a teacher in private and public schools nearly all the time from 1794 to 1845."[95]

Regardless of his or her identity, the Lexington-area teacher or teachers most likely moved from job to job and may have been engaged at several schools all within a short distance from Lexington. Mrs. Peabody, for example, who gave classes in embroidery in Billerica, also taught in Andover; she later instructed in Salem. Other embroidery teachers, such as Mrs. Battelle, Mrs. Martine de L'Mery, and Mrs. Cranch and her daughters, followed the same pattern. Susanna Rowson herself, who came from an English theatrical background and was at the top of her profession, moved from place to place (Newton, Medford, Boston), as did her sister-in-law, Mrs. Haswell, who taught school with her.[96]

Another influence on the spread (and the retention) of the motif was that certain families seemed to dominate the client field in a given neighborhood. For example, Nathan Munroe of Lexington [checklist 46] was the brother of Mary Munroe [checklist 54] and the second cousin of Anna Munroe [checklist 53], whose daughter Eusebia Harrington (born 1776) married Joseph Underwood, the son of Mary Munroe Underwood [checklist 54]. Moreover, Nathan's and Anna's respective spouses, Elizabeth Harrington (born 1750) and Daniel Harrington (born 1739) were third cousins. This may help explain why the tree-of-life sampler embroidered by Dorcas Munroe in 1802 is virtually identical to the one embroidered by Anna Munroe's granddaughter Lucebia Windship in 1812.[97] The Munroe, Harrington, and Mulliken families of Lexington accounted for about one-third of all the known samplers produced by the Lexington-area teacher or teachers.[98] In Waltham, each of two sisters in the Hagar family[99] was the subject of a Lexington-area record. It may be that the preceptress or preceptor responsible was a member of one of these families. Elsewhere, the J. P. artist seems to have had familial ties to his or her presumed clients and recorded an intermarriage between two children from each family register he or she made in Maine: Amos B. Pearson married Charlotte Matthews in 1805, and George Matthews wed Mariah Pearson two years later. Without going into detail, the same might be said of the Tarr, Parsons, and Lane families in Rockport or the Folger, Paddock, and Gardner families in Nantucket who accounted for many of the family records in their own communities.[100]

Fruits of the Tree of Life

Figure 123 [checklist 85]. John K. / Olive K. family tree. Thought to be a calligrapher's model. Watercolor. Circa 1825.

Figure 124 [checklist 92]. Asa K / Sally Blake (calligrapher's model). "We Ware Marrid. Feb 15 1817." Attributed to Joseph Odiorne. Watercolor. Pittsfield or Gilmanton, New Hampshire, circa 1825. Courtesy of Mr. and Mrs. Peter H. Tillou.

Figure 125 [checklist 42]. Thomas Sylvester / Polly Lane family tree.
Perhaps used as a model by the artist. Signed: "William Saville scripsit."
Watercolor. Gloucester, Massachusetts. Image courtesy of Skinner, Inc.,
www.skinnerinc.com.

The Role of Calligraphers and Embroidery Teachers

Figure 126 [checklist 19]. David Paddock / Mary Starbuck family tree. Watercolor. Nantucket, Massachusetts, circa 1834. Location unknown. Photograph provided by Nantucket Historical Association in 1987.

Fruits of the Tree of Life

Family Trees as "Living" Documents

The owners of an embroidered family register possessed what in effect was a finished artifact. Sewn work was usually difficult to change, obscure, or erase—or even to supplement—and in any case it meant altering the stitched testament left by a female predecessor. Few additions were made to them, and few were changed.[101] With watercolors it was an entirely different story; they were construed or conceived of as living memorials. While it is impossible to provide a log of all corrections, additions, and different handwriting on watercolor family records—some done years later perhaps by grown children, other relatives, or subsequent owners—there are hardly any watercolor examples in the group we are considering that have not been added to, overwritten, modified, or otherwise altered.

In some instances, the entire document seems dedicated to the future. When Eunice Gardner put together the three-stem family register marking births and deaths of the larger Gardner/Paddack, Cartwright/Bunker, Cartwright/Gardner [checklist 8] families of Nantucket, she left two empty white flags in an underused area and an extra blank rosebud to allow subsequent relatives to fill these out as it became necessary. The same pattern dominated other Nantucket pieces. The maker of the Myrick/Mitchell tree [checklist 17] prepared a broken and discolored banner held by a bird to mark a possible death; it, too, was never used. The maker of the Pent/Ripley tree [checklist 15] made three bird-supported banners that were completed, however. Other examples pertain to the eight children born to Abbe Jaquith and Abigail Whiting [checklist 83], who are celebrated in a family tree that provided unfilled husks for recording the deaths of the children. These blanks now contain as much genealogical information as the birth apples themselves, as new data were added to the Jaquith piece by several other hands years afterwards, some as late as 1901. This was a typical purpose of these registers: to keep a living memorial of the parents and children who had passed away. Sometimes these updates were added whether or not there was room aesthetically. The beautifully composed Hiller/Smith [checklist 5] family tree documenting the Nantucket births of eight children is "impaired" by the later addition of a ninth child (Edwin Hiller) in handwriting completely different from that of Edward D. Burke; the final pod is drawn asymmetrically, even crudely, and almost goes off the left-hand edge of the piece. But it made good sense to the Hiller family. In fact, the deaths of all the children are placed carefully below each pod, just above the rose blossom, in what appear to be three different handwriting styles. The family register was not "completed" until 1874 when Elizabeth Hiller died at the age of 87 on 4 March of that year and a relative added that last piece of data.

As is often the case in genealogical cataloging, this updating by later generations led to other anomalies. The original portion of the watercolor Charles Folger / Judith Coffin family tree [checklist 16] was scripted in 1827 with a finely prepared black ink that carefully provided the month, day, and year of each birth, enclosing each name in a yellow oval or pink heart. A later relative, however, working between 1850 and 1893, used a pencil (sometimes unsharpened) to record the deaths wherever there was room, sometimes crudely erasing mistakes or leaving last-minute calculations to determine what year was involved.

In some cases, too, there was an attempt to erase or obliterate both the text and even some of the artwork. Occasionally these changes were superficial. Of the eight apples hanging on the Clement/Pierce family tree [checklist 79], only two are suspended on attached stems. Five have been separated, leaving spots of bleached ink; one apple never had a stem. The most likely explanation is that someone kept the piece "up to date" with the deaths of the children and wanted to separate fruit from the branch. The same process is seen more distinctly on the Paddock/Starbuck watercolor (*Figure 126*) [checklist 19], marking the 1801 marriage and six children of David Paddock and Mary Starbuck of Nantucket; it, too, is a relatively late work, done circa 1834 according to the final date in the original handwriting. The three top circles, which presumably list additional marriages and births, show distinct signs of ink or pigment removal, again either by water or other bleaching agent, making the writing barely visible. We can reconstruct the text of the upper circle through the help of genealogies; the missing part reads: "David Paddock / married Eliza Russell / August 31 1845."[102] Eliza was David's second wife, aged 54 at the time of their marriage; he was 67. We do not know the circumstances regarding this match, but it appears that a later owner of the register, possibly one of the children of the earlier Paddock/Starbuck marriage, simply removed their names perhaps because he or she disapproved of the marriage.

A similar instance took place with a Gloucester-made family tree, and here we have a better sense, though still incomplete, of the family circumstances that precipitated it. The Channel/Burnham, Channel/Cleveland, Channel/Cox family tree (*Figure 127*) [checklist 30], a piece composed and signed by William Saville in 1795, was collected by Nina Fletcher Little because of its Ipswich connections. (It is now part of the collections at Historic New England's Cogswell's Grant.) The unusual story behind it begins in England, when Abraham Channel was ostensibly born in 1748 as Abraham Filch in Shefford, Bedfordshire. As a young man he was seized by a British Navy impressment crew while serving as an apprentice tailor in London. After several cruises, he escaped service when the ship he was held on was taken by an American privateer. He changed his name to Abraham Fitz-John Channel (Channel being his mother's maiden name), and switching sides, he fought against the English in the Revolution. After his retirement from maritime service, he ended up in Ipswich's Chebacco Parish (now Essex, Massachusetts) where he opened an inn and tailoring shop, married Abagail (or Abigail) Burnham in 1779, and fathered six children born between 1780 and 1792. After Abagail died of consumption in 1794, Abraham married in 1795 Elizabeth Cleveland, daughter of Rev. John Cleveland of Chebacco, and relocated to nearby Weare, New Hampshire, where on 4 November 1796 they had a daughter named Mary Cleveland (1796–1830). Abraham apparently abandoned this marriage and in 1807 wed Mary Dyer Smith of Boston (with whom he had one child named Susan, born in January 1809). When Mary Smith's husband, Capt. Stephen Smith (who had been "missing at sea") returned, this marriage was annulled. Although she and Abraham had been married for less than a month, Mary continued to use her married name Channel; she and her daughter entered the Shaker Community at Harvard, Massachusetts, where they are buried. Abraham Channel subsequently married in 1814 Welthy or Wealthy Cox, of Hanover, New Hampshire, as his fourth wife, and moved to Lake Memphremagog, Quebec, Canada, where he opened a hotel and fathered at least three more children. He died in Quebec at the reputed age of 110, his long life credited to "uniform habits of temperance."[103]

Between the year Abagail Burnham died in 1794 and Abraham's marriage to Elizabeth Cleveland on 1 January 1795, Abraham Channel and other Ipswich residents presumably commissioned William Saville to paint a memorial for Abagail (*Figure 128*). This was followed a few months later by the family register dated 10 July 1795 by Saville, which named his six children and his new wife Elizabeth. This document appears to have remained untouched through one subsequent marriage in 1807 to Mary Dyer Smith until Abraham wed Welthy Cox in 1814. At this point someone (perhaps it was Welthy herself) mostly obliterated Elizabeth Cleveland's name and birth date of 1757 and substituted Welthy's name just below it, as well as her marriage date to Abraham of 1 June 1814 and her birth date of 18 December 1782. Three of the four blank apples still remaining at the top of the tree were inscribed with the names and birth dates of Abraham and Welthy's three surviving children, Susan (born 1816), Leon (born 1818), and Stuart (born 1820); even though there was an available apple, neither Elizabeth's daughter, nor Mary's, was ever added.[104] In every sense of the word, the combined Channel/Burnham, Channel/Cleveland, and Channel/Cox family tree was a "living" document.

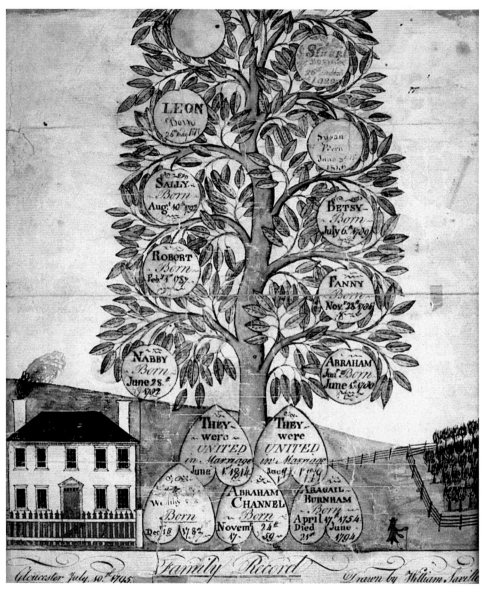

Figure 127 [checklist 30]. Abraham Channel / Abagail Burnham, Abraham Channel / Elizabeth Cleveland, Abraham Channel / Welthy Cox family register. Signed: "Drawn by William Saville." Gloucester, Massachusetts, 10 July 1795. Watercolor. Courtesy of Historic New England. Gift of Bertram K. and Nina Fletcher Little, 1991.1320.

Fruits of the Tree of Life

Figure 128. Memorial for Mrs. Abagail Channel of Ipswich (1754–1794), "dedicated by her Friends and Relations." Signed: "Drawn by William Saville." Watercolor. Ipswich, Massachusetts, circa 1794. Courtesy of Historic New England. Gift of Bertram K. and Nina Fletcher Little, 1991.1319.

Figure 129 [checklist 28]. James Parsons / Deborah Lane, James Parsons / Patience Knights family trees. Signed: "William Saville." Watercolor. Gloucester, Massachusetts, circa 1795–1800. Courtesy of Historic New England. Gift of Constance McCann Betts, Helena Woolworth Guest and Frasier W. McCann, 1942.2589.2.

Fruits of the Tree of Life

Didactic and Legal Uses of Family Registers

Although we do not always know what motivation lay behind these attempts to modify watercolor documents, we do know that most family registers were designed primarily for private viewing in the owners' household. The Jaquith/Whiting record in Ashby [checklist 83] was said by one family descendant to have been folded and just stored away in a desk or box.[105] This may have been typical since many of these watercolor registers show marks of being folded, and in ten the folding is prominent. (These lines are particularly visible when a piece is later framed, and some examples have broken on the ridges.) Sometimes, however, these documents might also have been seen by the public. We know that Avis Stearns Van Wagenen examined the framed family tree in the Stearns household in the last decade of the nineteenth century when visiting a relative in her ancestral home in Billerica. John B. Copp's family tree "hung in the Copp family home in Stonington, Connecticut" during the first half of the nineteenth century. Other descendants did the same, including one who reported that the Coffin/Folger [checklist 18] record was framed "and for many years hung over the fire place at the old homestead in Nantucket."[106]

Typically, too, the documents communicated didactic lessons and sayings drawn from well-known secular and biblical sources. One inscription on the 1816 Thomas Pinkham / Bridget Berry family tree reminds the reader, "Art thou a Son? or a Daugter [sic]?" [checklist 23]—a derivation from a spelling book issued by Noah Webster in Hartford, Connecticut, in 1787.[107] The inscription at the bottom of the document, "Be grateful to thy Father for He gave thee Life:...And to thy Mother, for She sustained thee," comes from the same passage in a 1787 English grammar by D. Fenning.[108] Their union was "Intermarried at New-Durham" and they pledged, "We Owe God Above Duty, Fealty, and Love." Their children were ushered in with the words "Unto Whom was born" as they were in Spencer/Buswel [checklist 100]—a biblical phrase probably derived from Luke 2:11. Some of these same maxims were also written with the genealogical records in the Pinkham family Bible.[109] Other calligraphers were less profuse but were equally concerned with family ties and remembrance. J. P.'s "Keep sacred the memory of your Ancestors" is inscribed on the tree trunk of both Pearson/Sevey [checklist 90] and Matthews/Chessley [checklist 89]. Trees attributed to Joseph Odiorne display the biblical "Peace be within thy walls & prosperity within thy palaces."[110] Another hoped "Ye Guardians" (probably meaning the parents) would "with tender care this fruit protect from every snare" [Clement/Pierce, checklist 79].[111] The most common were simple declarative phrases such as "stillborn," or "a child . . . died," or "unto whom was born," or "have issue." For those men involved in the maritime trades, terms such as "drowned" or "lost at sea" also show up frequently.[112]

Occasionally these documents came to serve a legal purpose, usually to support the petition of a war veteran's widow to secure a government pension. Bridget Berry Pinkham, widow of Thomas Pinkham [checklist 23], used her register in a failed attempt[113] to acquire a pension on the basis of his having served in the Revolutionary forces in 1776 and again in 1782. To help establish her legal relationship to him, she had the register authenticated by a judge (Peter O. Thacher of the municipal court in Boston), who signed his name and position in the upper left-hand corner. Other examples include the family of Ebenezer Spencer [checklist 100], whose document is also held in the Revolutionary War Pension and Bounty-Land-Warrant Application files of the U.S. National Archives. Mehetabel Spencer's petition was successful; her appeal for a pension relied on her son's sworn statement that "the paper here annexed is the original family record of my father & mother . . . and has existed in the family ever Since my earliest recollection."[114] In another case, Abigail Jenkins, the destitute widow of John Jenkins—whose career as the founder of American penmanship teaching had been compromised by his imitators[115]— submitted her application for a widow's pension with a manuscript family record possibly executed by Jenkins himself.[116] Financial assistance was more important to these widows than retaining a sentimental family document.

While watercolors were sometimes offered as supportive evidence for widows requesting pensions, only a small number of embroideries were used for that purpose. As the scholar Aimee E. Newell points out in her study of needlework by aging women, Mary Hearn Fralick, a daughter of a Revolutionary War soldier, submitted a sampler she had embroidered as a young girl on Nantucket Island to the Records of the Veterans Administration to help document her parents' marriage. The request was delayed after inspectors found that some of the date's stitching and Mary's age had been reworked, but her mother eventually received her widow's pension.[117]

More commonly, the ultimate role of family records was to serve as prized documents passed down by successive owners to their descendants. This act of sharing within families prompted what may have been an assembly line of duplications in the recording sequence because copies were made for siblings and other relatives. The Chelsea, Massachusetts, artist Edward Pratt labeled the Cheever/Eustes tree [checklist 97] as "(No 3)," presumably the third in a succession of copies to be given to other Cheever or Eustes kinfolk at the time he made it in 1799. The handwriting of the three-family Gardner/Paddack, Cartwright/Bunker, Cartwright/Gardner tree done by Eunice Gardner in 1796 [checklist 8] appears to have been scribbled and may have been one of several that were quickly executed.

Any document that stressed this memorial role set in motion a chain of family remembrances that bridged generations. The same James Parsons (born 28 May 1786) whose birth was recorded in 1795 by William Saville in a double family register marking his father James Parsons's two marriages to Deborah Lane and Patience Knights (*Figure 129*) [checklist 28] reappears as the husband sixteen years later in another double watercolor, this time composed by Joshua Pool. A seaman, James Parsons drowned in 1808 and was remembered by the Goss family when his widow Tammy W. Goss married her second husband, Timothy R. Davis of Gloucester (*Figures 130 and 131*) [checklist 35]. Timothy Davis acquired one stepchild at the time of his marriage and was later the father to seven more children that included a son called James Parsons Davis, born in 1812. The same Solomon Robbards who was pictured as a child in Saville's Robards/Thurston family tree reappears as a parent in Pool's Robbards/Brown tree; his son Solomon reappears in Pool's memorial for the 14-year-old boy in 1819. In Lexington, John Mulliken, who is a child in an embroidered piece by Faustina Mulliken (*Figure 132*) [checklist 59] circa 1805–1810, later turns up as the husband of Susanna Reed in 1813 in a family register by Susan Mulliken dated around 1826 (*Figure 133*) [checklist 68].

This passion for remembrance sometimes led to duplications of the basic family information in a different style. The Sawyer/Wyman, Ryan/Wyman family register marking the marriage of Samuel Ryan and Polly Sawyer in Sharon, New Hampshire, was replicated by the next generation in a new format using two standing trees (*Figure 134*) [checklist 86], which produces a wholly different impression on the viewer. In fact, one of the earliest family registers in this entire series, Nantucket's Gardner/Beard piece [checklist 2], was redrawn (but using the same data) by another Nantucket hand (presumably a descendant) in an updated style (*Figure 135*) [checklist 21] in the late nineteenth or even in the early twentieth century. This suggests that the twin-heart motif was gradually shifting in owners' minds and served as much a marker of social standing or one of inheritance as it was a genealogical emblem. In this case, the copyist was apparently making sure that the Gardners and the Beards were seen as one of the early Nantucket families on the island.

Very rarely copies were also used as a means to update an extended genealogy. The second strawberry-themed Coffin/Folger piece (*Figure 136*) [checklist 22], given to the Nantucket Historical Association by the same descendant as the first (*Figure 54*) [checklist 18], used an expanded format of the first to enlarge it by three more generations. The initial subjects are Samuel Coffin (1746–1809) and Eunice Folger (1754–1838), who were married in Nantucket in 1774. The later nineteenth-

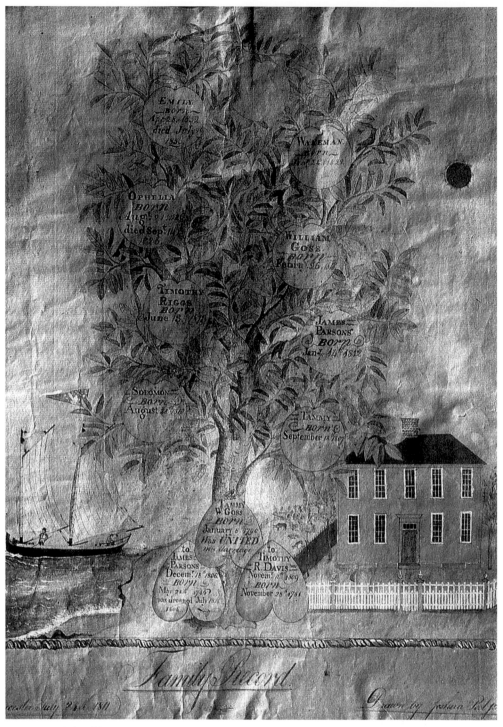

Figure 130 [checklist 35]. James Parsons / Tammy W. Goss, Timothy R. Davis / Tammy W. Goss family tree. Signed: "Gloucester July 24th 1811 Drawn by Joshua Pool Jr." Watercolor. Gloucester, Massachusetts, 1811. Sandy Bay Historical Society.

Fruits of the Tree of Life

century copy—reputedly made in October 1881 by John Newton Standish Jr. (who had married Samuel and Eunice's great-granddaughter)—adds three subsequent marriages, producing a "tree" containing four sets of parental hearts.[118] Thus, a second pair of hearts midway up the strawberry vine in the 1881 copy belongs to the Coffins' son John Gear Coffin and his wife Rebecca Luce Joy, who married in 1820. Their children, Benjamin Joy Coffin (born 1821), Kezia Joy Coffin (born 1825), and Mary Abby Coffin (1828–1918), are grandchildren of Samuel and Eunice. The third set of hearts higher up records the 1848 marriage of Mary Abby Coffin to George Riddell Simpson (1814–1864). The fourth or last level celebrates their daughter Mary Louise Pollard Simpson's 1878 union with John N. Standish Jr., who reputedly drew the piece.[119] Probably done at their home in Bridgeport, Connecticut, the watercolor carefully preserves the same format and some of the old punctuation of the first. Its "vertical" expansion of the twin-heart motif—unique not only by its strawberry theme but also because it encompasses the span of four generations—is the only known instance of this phenomenon in the visual annals of New England genealogy.[120]

Figure 131 [checklist 35]. Detail of James Parsons / Tammy W. Goss, Timothy R. Davis / Tammy W. Goss family tree.

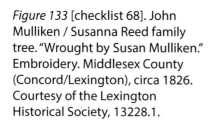

Figure 132 [checklist 59]. John Mulliken / Lydia Whiting family tree. "Faustina Mulliken's Work." Embroidery. Middlesex County, Massachusetts (Lexington/Concord), circa 1805–1810.

Figure 133 [checklist 68]. John Mulliken / Susanna Reed family tree. "Wrought by Susan Mulliken." Embroidery. Middlesex County (Concord/Lexington), circa 1826. Courtesy of the Lexington Historical Society, 13228.1.

Fruits of the Tree of Life

Figure 134 [checklist 86]. Josiah Sawyer / Patty Wyman, Samuel Ryan / Patty Wyman Sawyer family tree. Embroidery. "Wrought by Martha Ryan." Sharon or New Ipswich, New Hampshire. Circa 1820–1825. Image courtesy of M. Finkel & Daughter.

Figure 135 [checklist 21]. Ebenezer Gardner Jr. / Ruth Beard family tree. Watercolor. Nantucket, Massachusetts, late nineteenth or twentieth century? Courtesy of the Nantucket Historical Association Research Library, 1932.30.1. Gift of William F. Macy from the Estate of Lizzie Macy.

Fruits of the Tree of Life

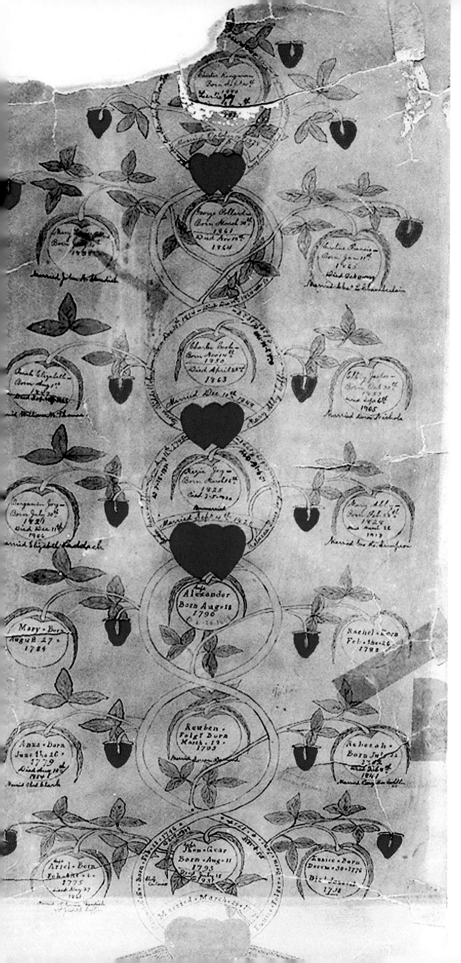

Figure 136
[checklist 22].
Samuel Coffin / Eunice
Folger family tree, with
three generations of
Coffin descendants
added above.
Watercolor. Nantucket,
Massachusetts,
or Bridgeport,
Connecticut, 1881.
Courtesy of the
Nantucket Historical
Association Research
Library, 2003.23.5.
Gift of Merwin Lodge.

Figure 137 [checklist 111]. Job Parke / Lucy Dey (Lucy New?) family tree. Copy of a family tree by William Richardson. Eastern United States, twentieth century, circa 1975. Photograph from *Masterpieces of American Folk Art* (1975).

The Impact of Forgeries

The gradual shift of family record ownership from successive generations to individual and institutional collections offers several new challenges—especially as many of these items are now traded by dealers and auction houses via electronic media and take advantage of the same growing body of data that has greatly assisted this present study. Under these circumstances, the emergence of counterfeits has been inevitable. Between 1975 and 2017 at least four potential forgeries and one possible imitation have either entered the market or have been exhibited in the public media. Of these, perhaps the most flagrant is a forged copy of William Richardson's Job Dennen / Lucy Gott (*Figure 69*) [checklist 41]. Simply put, the Job Parke / Lucy Dey family tree (*Figure 137*) [checklist 111] is a twentieth-century imitation of Richardson's piece done years before digital photography became common. The copyist masked his or her efforts by changing the two surnames but still retained most of the first names of the original as well as all the visual details. "Job Dennen" is now "Job Parke"; "Lucy Gott" becomes "Lucy Dey" (or "Lucy New"). The piece reproduces verbatim all three of the later death notices with their misspellings—for example, Richardson's "So fades the lovely blooming flour" is repeated word for word in the counterfeit. The item was exhibited at the Monmouth Museum in Lincroft, New Jersey, in a 1975 exhibition guest curated by the New York folk art dealer John Gordon and was featured in Robert Bishop's book on American folk art.[121] A second counterfeit is a watercolor copy of the family data appearing on an authentic embroidery signed by Eliza Meriam (*Figure 82*) [checklist 50], presently owned by the Lexington Historical Society. The watercolor copy of the data on this embroidery (*Figure 138*) [checklist 112] is crudely done and follows a "Gloucester" style and is ostensibly inscribed "Lexington, Mass., 1805 . . . by William Saville." Saville of course had no association with Lexington. This item was being circulated in eastern Massachusetts in the late 1980s and 1990s and was auctioned on 22 April 2007 as a "Circa 1900 watercolor on paper by William Saville"—forty-seven years after Saville's death.[122] Two other pieces [checklist 113 and 114] lack any credible labelling or provenance. They include a pot adorned with two hearts—a motif that seems similar to the image shown in *Figure 123* [checklist 85]—as well as a totally spurious representation of a Nantucket family tree.[123]

The above examples are, or seem to be, falsifications. But other family records suggest similar ambiguities. One of the most stunning examples of Saville's work is the family tree he made and signed for the Lane/Marchent family of Gloucester (*Figure 61*) [checklist 27]. (Its present location is unknown, but it was at one time in the collection of Howard and Catherine Feldman.) The Lane/Marchent register, however, has so many characteristics in common with one ostensibly signed by Saville for Gloucester's Sylvester/Lane's family (*Figure 125*) [checklist 42], it brings into question the latter's authenticity as a family register. The record displays two mansion houses side by side along with a profusion of patently unreadable names. On the face of it, Sylvester/Lane seems to be an almost exact copy of Lane/Marchent, including the style of architecture of the mansion houses, the vines crawling above the hearts, the heavy script of the upper apples, the tapered line below the signature, the shading of the tree trunk, and even the small period after the word "Record." The Sylvester family was not active in Gloucester until after 1830, so there is little documentary or genealogical confirmation to support a commissioned family tree. Yet the skilled artistic technique and the apparent age and repeated creasing of the paper suggest that the document may have been an artist's sample.

At the same time, the use of the internet also raises questions about a number of more accepted items in this genre. The watercolor of the Josiah Davis / Abigail Hubbard family—an important register that likely took the twin-heart concept from Lexington, Massachusetts, to New Ipswich, New Hampshire—is known from two photographs. In a recent image taken at an antiques show (*Figure 93*) [checklist 78], it appears in a reddish frame, but the piece seems so "retouched" it looks highly questionable. Further research, however, reveals an earlier image, apparently taken before restoration (*Figure 92*) [checklist 78], that was posted on the internet by another dealer in 2012. This time the piece is held in a wholly different (drab) frame; there is staining at the lower end of the watercolor, and the tree's bark has numerous breaks in it. The family tree is actually much more believable in this unretouched version. Unfortunately, we can expect to see many more compromised examples like this one.

Figure 138 [checklist 112]. Rufus Meriam / Martha Simonds family tree. Signed: "by William Saville." Watercolor. Eastern United States, twentieth-century copy of the data provided by a Middlesex County embroidery. Location unknown.

Conclusion: The Larger Picture

In retrospect, it is hard to escape the conclusion that the twin-heart and hearts-within-heart motifs may have been seen by most early nineteenth-century New Englanders as naive or as "infant specimens of Taste"—the latter being a term used by William Bentley when he first toured Cape Ann in 1799 and noticed William Saville's genealogical and memorial artwork.[124] It was the same assessment offered a hundred years later by the genealogist Avis Van Wagenen, who remembered that among the "treasured relics" in John Stearns's Billerica house was "a rude picture, representing the family-tree, with a heart-shaped apple to record each birth in the family of John and Mary (Lane) Stearns, married Feb. 10, 1800."[125]

Bentley's and Van Wagenen's assessments may have been entirely appropriate. The fruits and flowers of the "Tree of Life" seem to have proliferated among relatively unsophisticated and geographically secluded people of a larger population that always saw itself as provincial and was constantly trying to Europeanize its cultural perspective.[126] These remote families were articulating the thinking of an isolated element in the early American social hierarchy, not the society as a whole; many were members of seamen's families who lived in remote areas, such as Nantucket Island, Martha's Vineyard, and Cape Ann, or farming families inhabiting the thinly settled communities of northern Massachusetts, the New Hampshire foothills, and the small towns on the Maine coastline and inland Maine. It was no less of an observer than J. Hector St. John de Crèvecœur who noted in his *Letters from Nantucket and Martha's Vineyard* that he found

> a simplicity of diction and manners [among Nantucket residents], rather more primitive and rigid than I expected; and I soon perceived that it proceeded from their secluded situation, which has prevented them from mixing with others.[127]

Other makers of these documents were school children like those living in Newington, Connecticut, or in Newbury, Massachusetts, who grew up in the inexperience of youth in a rural environment. Drawings "Made by Anna Camp in January AD 1787" [checklist 104] or "Taken by Atkinson Stanwood" in

Newburyport in 1814 and 1816 [checklist 109 and 110] represented a child's point of view as it was seen from within an individual family's perspective. And most of the embroidered genealogies using the motif (which were generated in more densely populated communities and closer to urban areas) were stitched by girls aged 10 to 15, who were only doing what their parents and teachers wanted, that is, to promote themselves and memorialize their families.

All these characteristics were signs of persistent provincialism and regionalism that still encumbered the imagination of most Americans. If this point of view is accurate, the twin-heart genealogical motif may be metaphorically akin to the unique language characteristics uncovered by the linguist William Labov in his 1963 study of common speech on the islands of Martha's Vineyard and Nantucket. Labov found seventeenth-century pronunciation and lexical traditions among the old families of English stock ("studdled" for dirty water, "tempests" for storms, the retention of "r" in "barn"). He also found variations in pronunciation between one side of the island and the other.[128] And what was true of Martha's Vineyard (and presumably Nantucket) may also apply to other areas where the motif found favor—giving life to the claim by the late historian and genealogist Gregory H. Laing, who often joked to those using the Special Collections at the Haverhill Public Library that the most common given name for girls in Gloucester's Fifth Parish was Tammy or Tamma—as regional a name as one could find anywhere in New England.

A case can be made, too, that many of these documents were inspired largely through family ties. The Folger clan on Nantucket clearly had a key role in the evolution of the local island design and may have even engendered it. William Saville and his presumed brother-in-law Joshua Pool Jr. dominated the trade in Gloucester and basically limited their clients to a small number of local families. And the links found between the Munroe, Harrington, and Underwood families in Lexington—duplicated by comparable links between the Stearns, Davis, and Hubbard families in Ashburnham and New Ipswich—kept the Middlesex style (and their watercolor imitators) active among siblings, first cousins, second cousins, and third cousins. Clearly, the relationship between the appearance and retention of the twin-heart motif and these ties is not likely to be a coincidence.

But regardless of where the twin-heart motif originated, these artists were also tied to the nineteenth century and subject to changes in fashion. Shifts in the twin-heart design got "stronger" in the nineteenth century, as the idea permeated into relatively remote parts of federal America as part of its inherited culture. The tentatively executed images seen in the 1790s in Nantucket and Gloucester as well as in Middlesex County at the beginning of the fifty-year period in some ways seem to have responded to local influences even as the image reached its height in the period 1810 to 1820. In doing so, the designs underwent a change. The slender climbing rose stems and vines shown in Gardner/Beard [2] and Cartwright/

Gardner [8] had become a substantial vine by the time another artist composed the Nathaniel Starbuck tree [12]. In Gloucester, small apple trees had increased in size, and the trunks and lower limbs thickened in the hands of Saville and Pool. In one instance the images have turned into hardened oaks. In Martha Ryan's embroidery of her mother's two marriages to Josiah Sawyer and Samuel Ryan (*Figure 134*) [checklist 86] the trees are so sturdy that the genealogical data almost get lost in a busy landscape. Fruits also seem to undergo a change. Martha's embroidered fruits appear so heavy they seem to be drooping to the ground. She records a death with a fallen fruit (a rarity); and then she boldly adds her own name on the ground announcing she had "wrought" the sampler.

As nineteenth-century decorative tastes seeped into the design, other fruits or flowers changed as well. The names of children on the Pinkham/Berry image, dated 1816, are closely enclosed in leaves—almost like a hazel nut—with a characteristic clump of foliage attached at the top. The same decorative touch appears on the fruits of the Alexander/Dicson tree, where each child's name is encapsulated with a protective cover. It also emerges, incidentally, on the only twin-heart image found in the upper Connecticut River Valley, the Wheeler/Goodnow tree [checklist 81] whose children are virtually surrounded by large leaves. Both examples may represent a late manifestation in nineteenth-century decorative taste that seems to have flourished in the 1830s and 1840s.

But even as it was regional, the twin-heart motif was also more individualistic than most printed or school-taught family trees created in early America. The majority of decorated New England registers, especially those that have accumulated in institutional collections, feature building-related themes and display tablatures. They tend to be "architectural" and "sepulchral" in their format and in a larger sense emphasize the stability of the home where the family flourished and its nearby gravesite—rather than the emotions that bound individual families together. This architectural format, which usually involves pillars, cornices, columns, arched bridges, chains, or even rigid lists of names, allowed calligraphers to put children into neat vertical rows arranged by dates and to adorn them with classic or federal symbols of family. We think of designs chosen by engravers and printers like Richard Brunton, Justus Dalee, and Rufus Porter, whose idealized figures of Faith, Hope, Charity, and Peace were seen as promoting stability and permanence—the graphic equivalent of unmovable slate or marble gravestones and mausoleum fronts. We also think of genealogical artists from other ethnic backgrounds such as Isaac N. Cardozo, a Jewish immigrant from London living in Philadelphia, who composed elaborate family registers that were "Cemented With Love" that used symbols of time, arched bridges, keystones, arithmetical equations, compasses, and celestial figures amidst an array of children's names.[129]

In the end the twin-heart and heart-within-heart themes discussed here tend to be more visually inclusive, personal, and engaging; they often involve horticultural elements—earth mounds, tree trunks, vines, and flowers—whose lines, stamens, and tendrils trace the children's parentage with considerable precision. Former marriages and their spouses and their children are recognized; deaths are marked with withered, separated, or discolored flowers or fruits or cut-off stems ending without issue. These documents frequently record other personal details. Household, maritime, and agricultural objects are woven into the design: farming equipment for Edward Pratt's Chelsea register, fishing smacks and sailboats for Joshua Pool's Gloucester registers; fishermen's and sea captains' residences for William Saville's work; wild-growing *Rosa rugosa* for Phebe Folger's, Edward D. Burke's, and Daniel Stanton's registers; and cultivated strawberries for the maker of the Coffin/Folger register.

This pattern may account for the critical difference between the New England group and the multi-heart family registers by Pennsylvania and rural New York calligraphists, which have been so skillfully collected and studied by Arthur B. and Sybil B. Kern.[130] The colored "Fraktur" tradition of William Murray (1756–1828), Samuel Morton (active 1804–1809), and Henry Moyer (active 1819–1825) and their schools frequently show the same basic depictions of multi-heart images and of a tulip "coming out of" a heart in the late eighteenth and early nineteenth centuries. But these designs were a long-existing tradition and do not possess the immediacy communicated by the New England artists described here. The Fraktur calligraphers responsible for them had a ready market for their work, despite their standing outside the "English" decorating tradition. By contrast, the New England calligraphers, such as the Folgers, Edward D. Burke, William Saville, and Joshua Pool Jr., and the Lexington- and Taunton-area embroidery teachers, had to create a market. Even individual artists like J. P. and Eunice Gardner may have been obliged to generate one in order to have their work accepted by the community. The Fraktur influence itself came intact from Europe in the eighteenth-century and was reproduced quickly in the southeastern portion of Pennsylvania where Germans predominated. Its calligraphy already had a style divisible into a dozen or more areas of concentration which the artists tried to duplicate; in other words, it was a recognized language and a script instead of a hypothesized one. At least one Fraktur artist in Pennsylvania preprinted what appear to have been hundreds of heart illustrations containing legalistic genealogical language within the heart. A printer or bookseller would add his or her clients' names to the written part and then apply colors to decorate the printed heart in a special design. The "fast-track" approach to this work depended on having scores of customers. To Phebe Folger and Eunice Gardner and J. P. and their colleagues, however, composing registers was an act of regional and personal remembrance.

Beyond these considerations is the issue of cultural patterning. While the four-generation reach of the late nineteenth-century strawberry design composed for Nantucket's Coffin family and the intricate lover's knot joining the hearts of J. P.'s family trees are both striking, it is the Pinkham/Berry [checklist 23] family tree of New Durham, New Hampshire, and the related register of the Alexander/Dicson family [checklist 24] of Webster Plantation, Maine, that end up being two of the most important "finds" among family records over the last three decades. Both speak to competing suppositions about the origins of their motif. On the one hand, they suggest that the unusual vine variant (which this author previously believed had been restricted to Nantucket Island and Martha's Vineyard) had in fact broken away from its confinement and was thriving along New Hampshire's and Maine's inland towns that had access (if sometimes limited) to the sea. One group in New England had somehow communicated and passed along its household language of genealogical memories to another, many miles away. This was a cultural leap that draws attention and suggests that "regional" expressions and styles could travel long distances.

On the other hand, the two pieces may actually convey the opposite. Although the Nantucket and Maine designs have some similarities, there is evidence that they may not derive from each other because both the Pinkham and Alexander vines are punctuated with a star where they intersect. By contrast, none of the Nantucket vines has that star or any semblance of such a star. This suggests the artists and calligraphers responsible in Nantucket Island and Martha's Vineyard and those in Maine were not in touch with each other and instead were drawing on the same widely shared "visual language" or "dialect" still persisting among the early English and other European immigrants to New England, who in effect had brought over this taste from Europe. If the Pinkham/Berry and Alexander/Dicson records really were a Nantucket / Martha's Vineyard subgroup, the artists would likely have preserved "Nantucket" features just as Sarah Rodman and John Brown Copp did in the first decades of the nineteenth century. But they did not and instead added a star or daisy flower where the vines cross. It is possible that, like the Nantucketers, the New Hampshire and Maine makers were still under the influence of the old royal genealogies—Benjamin Wright's 1603 "Roiail Progenei of our Most Sacred King Iames" or John Goddard's 1639 to 1650 "The Tree of Mans Life"—and created a new manifestation of a wider Atlantic or Euro-Atlantic style of genealogical conceptualizing. In the final analysis, it may have been only a coincidence that this twin-heart motif, which had ripened in areas such as Nantucket Island and Martha's Vineyard in the 1780s, was again resurrected in underpopulated areas of New Hampshire and the upriver Maine estuaries in the 1820s. Both of them were isolated and both produced or attracted gifted untaught artists that drew on old ideas.

Appendix:
Checklist of Twin-Heart and Multi-heart Family Registers

Second or third marriages listed on a given family register are not given new numbers. The abbreviation "do." stands for "ditto." Sources for checklist items are found on p. 185.

Nantucket Type

	Father	Mother	Date of Marriage	Children	Location of Parents
1	Zaccheus Coffin (1751–1788)	Thankful Joy (1749–1810)	22 March 1770	1771–1780	Nantucket
2	Ebenezer Gardner Jr. (1732–1778)	Ruth Beard (1733–1823)	21 November 1751	1752–1770	Nantucket
3	Walter Folger (1734–1826)	Elizabeth Starbuck (1738–1821)	13 January 1757	1758–1778	Nantucket
4	Samuel Copp (1743–1820)	Dolley Brown (1744–1821)	10 December 1769	1770–1787	Nantucket / Stonington, Conn.
5	Thomas Hiller (1761–1839)	Elizabeth Smith (1763–1837)	3 November 1784	1785–1805	Nantucket
6	Obed Marshall (1744–1817)	Susanna Burnell (1747–1814)	12 February 1767	1767–1787	Nantucket
7	Obadiah Wood (1756–1825)	Martha Tupper (1762–1846)	20 January 1784	1785–1802	Nantucket
8	Peter Gardner (1754–1776)	Abigail Paddack (1757–1842)	12 May 1776	no children	Nantucket
8	Benjamin Cartwright (1748–1812)	Elizabeth Bunker (1754–1787)	29 October 1772	1772–1783	Nantucket
8	Benjamin Cartwright (1748–1812)	Abigail Paddack Gardner (1757–1842)	24 April 1788	1789–1799	Nantucket
9	John Stanton Kinyon (1767–1842)	Hannah Westcott (1767–1842)	October 1791	1792–1804	North Kingston, R.I. / Hopkinton, R.I.
10	Samuel Rodman (1753–1835)	Elizabeth Rotch (1757–1856)	1 June 1780	1781–1794	Nantucket / New Bedford
11	Crispus Gardner (1742–1805)	Margaret Chase (1743–1823)	8 December 1768	1769–1782	Nantucket
12	Nathaniel Starbuck (1745–1812)	Eunice Barnard (1749–1775)	30 October 1765	1767–1774	Nantucket
12	Nathaniel Starbuck (1745–1812)	Salley [Sarah] Fullenton [Fullington] (1745–1777)	2 January 1777	no living children	Nantucket
12	Nathaniel Starbuck (1745–1812)	Patience Coffin (1749–1827)	20 September 1778	1779–1781	Nantucket

Date of Record	Maker	Image Type / Dimensions	Owner/Dealer
ca. 1788	"Nantucket / Drawn by Phebe Folger"	Watercolor 8 1/2 x 6 1/2 in.	NHA 1927.28.1
ca. 1788 ?		Watercolor 18 3/8 x 13 3/8 in.	NHA 1932.30.2
ca. 1789–1800		Watercolor 18 1/2 x 15 1/2 in.	NHA 1905.29.2
ca. 1810–1815	"John B. Copp Pinxit"	Watercolor 20 1/2 x 17 1/8 in.	Smithsonian 28810
1794–1795	"Edw'd D. Burke, Pinxit"	Watercolor 12 9/16 x 11 1/2 in.	NHA 1968.10.6
1794–1796	"Edw'd D. Burke, Pin[xit]"	Watercolor	Paul Madden
1797–1802	"Edw'd D. B[ ]" "Edwd D. Burke, Pinxit"	Watercolor 10.5 x 8.25 in.	Location unknown; ex collection Charles Carpenter
1796	"Dron by Eunice Gardner 1796"	Watercolor 18 3/8 x 14 1/4 in.	NHA 1904.35.1
do.	do.	do.	do.
do.	do.	do.	do.
1796	"Drawn by Daniel S. Stant[on] 1796"	Watercolor 13 x 10 3/4 in.	Location unknown
ca. 1810	Sarah Rodman (attribution) Upper left: "Not correct"	Watercolor 12 1/2 x 16 in.	Private collection
1810–1820	"Daniel Stanton Pinxit"	Watercolor 13.5 x 12.5 in.	Ex collection Robert Cary Caldwell
1812	"E[unice ?] 1812"	Watercolor 13.5 x 12.5 in.	Location unknown
do.	do.	do.	do.
do.	do.	do.	do.

	Father	Mother	Date of Marriage	Children	Location of Parents
13	Alexander Folger (1773–1846)	Rebecca Folger (1778–1823)	9 May 1800	1801–1813	Nantucket
14	Edward Cary (1738–1812)	Lydia Barnard (1745–1814)	12 November 1770	1771–1789	Nantucket
15	Samuel Pent (1777–1841)	Deborah Ripley (1780–1870)	24 November 1805	1806–1823	Martha's Vineyard
16	Charles Folger (1779–1860)	Judith Coffin (1785–1850)	15 December 1803	1804–1824	Nantucket
17	George Myrick Jr. (1790–1863)	Eliza Mitchell (1791–1864)	7 September 1815	1816–1829	Nantucket
18	Samuel Coffin (1746–1809)	Eunice Folger (1754–1838)	8 March 1774 (int.)	1775–1790	Nantucket
19	David Paddock (1778–1856)	Mary Starbuck (1779–1842)	25 July 1801	1807–1816	Nantucket
20	William Barnard Coffin (1781–1867)	Deborah Swain (1784–1841)	4 April 1804	1804–1825	Nantucket
21	Ebenezer Gardner Jr. (1732–1778)	Ruth Beard (1733–1823)	21 November 1751	1752–1770	Nantucket
22	Samuel Coffin (1746–1809)	Eunice Folger (1754–1838)	8 March 1774 (int.)	1775–1790	Nantucket
22	John Gear Coffin (1795–1831)	Rebecca Luce Joy (1798–1894)	4 September 1820	1825–1828	Nantucket
22	George Riddell Simpson (1814–1864)	Mary Abby Coffin (1828–1918)	10 December 1848	1850–1861	Nantucket
22	John N. Standish Jr. (1856–1931)	Mary Louise Pollard Simpson (b. 1858)	10 October 1878	1880–1883	Nantucket / Bridgeport, Conn.

Mass., N.H., and Maine Variants of Nantucket Type

	Father	Mother	Date of Marriage	Children	Location of Parents
23	Thomas Pinkham (1752–1820)	Bridget Berry (1761–1846)	16 July 1782	1784–1804	New Durham, N.H. / Lebanon, Me.
24	Thomas Alexander (1769–1844)	Betsey Dicson (b. ca. 1770)	1 April 1798	1798–1818	Webster Plantation, Me.

Saville, Pool, and Richardson in Gloucester

	Father	Mother	Date of Marriage	Children	Location of Parents
25	William Rowe (1761–1824)	Betsy Dennison (1762–1843)	28 July 1782	1782–1806	Gloucester
26	Thomas Robards [Robbins] (1733–1818)	Dorcas Thurston (1739–1825)	27 October 1756	1758–1776	Ipswich / Gloucester

Date of Record	Maker	Image Type / Dimensions	Owner/Dealer
ca. 1813–1820		Watercolor 18 1/2 x 15 1/2 in.	NHA 1905.29.1
ca. 1800–1815		Watercolor H. 14 in.	Location unknown
ca. 1823–1830		Watercolor	Ex collection Pam Boynton / Location unknown
ca. 1827		Watercolor	Location unknown
ca. 1829		Watercolor 18 x 15 in.	NHA 1925.8.20
ca. 1831 ?		Watercolor 11 x 9 in.	NHA 2003.23.6
ca. 1834 ?		Watercolor	Location unknown
ca. 1830–1835		Watercolor H. 18 in.	Location unknown
Late 19th or 20th century?		Watercolor 17 1/2 x 14 1/2 in.	NHA 1932.30.1
1881	"The balance was added by J. N. Standish, Jr., Oct 1881."	Watercolor 22 x 10 in.	NHA 2003.23.5
do.		do.	do.
do.		do.	do.
do.		do.	do.

Date of Record	Maker	Image Type / Dimensions	Owner/Dealer
30 December 1816		Watercolor	Revolutionary War Pension . . . Application File
ca. 1830–1850		Watercolor	Location unknown

Date of Record	Maker	Image Type / Dimensions	Owner/Dealer
ca. 1793 ?	"William Saville Glocester September 17[ ]"	Watercolor	Sandy Bay Historical Society, 637
1793?	Attributed to William Saville	Watercolor 14 1/4 x 11 3/4 in.	Location unknown

	Father	Mother	Date of Marriage	Children	Location of Parents
27	David Lane (1750–1825)	Hannah Marchent (1752–1840)	12 November 1772	1774–1793	Gloucester
28	James Parsons (1745–1796)	Deborah Lane (1745–1785)	17 December 1768	1769–1780	Gloucester
28	James Parsons (1745–1796)	Patience Knights (b. 1762)	4 July 1785	1786–1793	Gloucester
29	John Woodbury (1739–1790)	Susanna Lane (1744–1823)	8 February 1762	1762–1787	Gloucester
30	Abraham Fitz-John Channel (1748–1858)	Abagail Burnham (1754–1794)	4 January 1779	1780–1792	Ipswich
30	Abraham Fitz-John Channel (1748–1858)	Elizabeth Cleveland (1757–1828)	1 January 1795	1796	Weare, N.H.
30	Abraham Fitz-John Channel (1748–1858)	Mary Dyer Smith (1764–1855)	16 November 1807, annulled 6 December 1807	1809	Boston
30	Abraham Fitz-John Channel (1748–1858)	Welthy Cox (1782–1862)	1 June 1814	1816–1820	Lake Memphremagog, Que.
31	Ebenezer Grover (1769–1839)	Sally Tarr (b. 1773)	11 March 1792	1793–1800	Gloucester
32	Nathaniel Griffin Jr. (1766–1807)	Priscilla Lane (1768–1855)	15 November 1789	1792–1806	Gloucester
33	Joseph Hicks (1778–1823)	Susanna Parsons (1782–1854)	21 November 1803	1804–1823	Gloucester
34	Jabez Tarr (1759–1844)	Peggy Somes (1765–1827)	2 December 1782	1784–1809	Gloucester
35	James Parsons (1786–1808)	Tammy W. Goss (1790–1879)	18 December 1806	1807	Gloucester
35	Timothy R. Davis (1781–1848)	Tammy W. Goss (1790–1879)	11 November 1809	1810–1832	Gloucester
36	James Dennison (1770–1858)	Thomasin Griffin (1777–1839)	14 November 1799	1800–1818	Gloucester
37	Solomon Robbards (b. 1771)	Polly Brown (b. 1777)	25 November 1802	1803–1816	Gloucester
38	Andrew Bickford (1783–1869)	Olive Clark (1790–1882)	1 December 1808	1810–1828	Gloucester
39	Felix Doyle (1794–1824)	Tamma Clark (1796–1839)	18 March 1816	1816–1824	Gloucester
40	Benjamin Colbey (1792–ca.1858)	Lois Tarr (1797–1869)	25 December 1816	1817–1837	Gloucester
41	Job Dennen (b. 1790)	Lucy Gott (1796–1853)	1 June 1817	1817–1838	Gloucester

Date of Record	Maker	Image Type / Dimensions	Owner/Dealer
1791–1793	"William Saville Scripsit"	Watercolor	Ex collection Howard and Catherine Feldman
ca. 1795–1800	"by William Saville"	Watercolor	Historic New England 1942.2589.2
do.	do.	do.	do.
1795	"Gloucester April 30th 1795 / Drawn by William Saville"	Watercolor	Cape Ann Museum
1795	"Gloucester July 10th. 1795. / Drawn by William Saville"	Watercolor 12 1/2 x 10 3/4 in.	Historic New England 1991.1320
do.	do.	do.	do.
do.	do.	do.	do.
do.	do.	do.	do.
1801	"Gloucester May 6th 1801 / Drawn by William Saville"	Watercolor	Historic New England, Beauport collection
1807	"Drawn by William Saville"	Watercolor	Location unknown
1808	"Gloucester April 4th / 1808"? "Drawn by Joshua P[ool]"	Watercolor	Location unknown
ca. 1809–1814	Attributed to Joshua Pool Jr.	Watercolor	Sandy Bay Historical Society, 638
1811	"Gloucester July 24 1811 / Drawn by Joshua Pool Jr."	Watercolor	Sandy Bay Historical Society
do.	do.	do.	do.
1815	"Gloucester April 4th 1815 / Taken by William Saville"	Watercolor	Cape Ann Museum
1819	"Drawn by J. Pool."	Watercolor	Location unknown
ca. 1828	"Done by J. Pool"	Watercolor 15 x 12 in.	American Folk Art Museum Accession: 1998.17.6
ca. 1821	Attributed to Joshua Pool, Jr.	Watercolor	Sandy Bay Historical Society, 636
ca. 1824	Attributed to Joshua Pool, Jr.	Watercolor	Sandy Bay Historical Society, 639
1838	"By Wm. Richardson"	Watercolor	Ex collection Mr. & Mrs. Erving Wolf

	Father	Mother	Date of Marriage	Children	Location of Parents
42	Thomas Sylvester	Polly Lane	?	?	Gloucester ?
43	[Tarr: Blank tree with hearts]				Gloucester

Middlesex County School[s] for Young Women

	Father	Mother	Date of Marriage	Children	Location of Parents
44	David Townsend (1745–1814)	Sarah Jenison (1748–1814)	23 November 1773	1775–1789	Watertown/Waltham
45	Thaddeus Davis (b. 1754)	Sarah Stearns (1759–1807)	28 September 1779	1780–1796	Bedford/Billerica
46	Nathan Munroe (1747–1829)	Elizabeth Harrington (1750–1812)	3 October 1769	1769–1793	Lexington
47	Benjamin Wellington (1743–1812)	Martha Ball (1745–1830)	4 December 1766	1767–1787	Lexington
48	John Clark (1766–1850)	Lydia Sanderson (1769–1862)	14 May 1793	1794–1805	Waltham
49	Abel Wyman (b. 1747)	Ruth Putnam (1751–1812)	20 October 1772	1773–1791	Woburn/Burlington
50	Rufus Meriam (1762–1847)	Martha Simonds (1766–1840)	23 August 1785	1787–1804	Lexington
51	Solomon Harrington (b. 1765)	Hannah Pierce (b. 1770)	26 April 1796	1797–1804	Waltham
52	Abraham Fisk (1773–1812)	Grace Hagar (b. 1774)	20 November 1794	1796–1811	Waltham
53	Daniel Harrington (1739–1818)	Anna Munroe (1740–1811)	3 May 1760	1760–1780	Lexington
54	Joseph Underwood (1749–1829)	Mary Munroe (1750–1802)	21 March 1771	1772–1790	Lexington
55	Nathan Russell (1760–1848)	Sybil Blood (1765–1853)	18 June 1795	1796–1808	Lexington
56	Robert Parker (1771–1840)	Elizabeth Simonds (1772–1849)	25 October 1793	1794–1817	Lexington
57	Francis Bright (1766–1828)	Susannah Bright (1778–1870)	27 December 1797	1798–1818	Watertown
58	William Stone (1781–1856)	Elizabeth Coolidge (1784–1874)	9 April 1807	1808–1818	Watertown
59	John Mulliken (1754–1840)	Lydia Whiting (1757–1825)	13 June 1780	1781–1793	Lexington/Concord
60	Samuel Barnes (1750–1799)	Grace Warren (1756–1831)	22 October 1774	1775–1794	Waltham
61	Joseph Garfield (1761–1824)	Susanna Hagar (1769–1857)	4 April 1787	1788–1811	Waltham

Fruits of the Tree of Life

Date of Record	Maker	Image Type / Dimensions	Owner/Dealer
?	"William Saville scripsit"	Watercolor	Location unknown
1800–1830	Tarr calculation book	Watercolor	John McInnis, Amesbury (auctioneer)

ca. 1790		Embroidery 15 x 8 1/4 in.	Concord Museum, Acc. T8
ca. 1800		Embroidery	Sandy Macfarlane
ca. 1802	"The Family Record Dorcas Munroe's Work" (b. 1788)	Embroidery 17 1/2 x 13 in.	Fine Arts Museums of San Francisco, 78.19.1
ca. 1801	Patty [Martha] Wellington (1785–1846)	Embroidery 20 x 15 1/2 in.	Lexington Historical Society, 12968
ca. 1807	"Alice Clark's Work."	Embroidery 15 3/4 x 12 1/2 in.	Location unknown
1807	"The Family Record Lucy P. Wyman's work/1807" (b. 1791)	Embroidery	Location unknown
ca. 1810	"The Family Record Eliza Meriam's Work" (b. 1793)	Embroidery 16 3/4 x 12 1/2 in.	Lexington Historical Society, 7317
ca. 1810–1815	"Family Record Ruth Harringtons" (b. 1799)	Embroidery 14 3/4 x 11 1/2 in.	Location unknown
1811	"Lorenza Fisk Work" (b. 1796)	Embroidery 18 1/2 x 16 1/4 in.	Winterthur Museum, 1969.430
ca. 1812	"Lucebia Windship's Work" (b. 1794)	Embroidery 20 x 13 1/2 in.	Lexington Historical Society, 12913
ca. 1810–1830	"The Family Record Mary M. Smith Work" (b. 1798)	Embroidery 17 3/4 x 16 1/4 in.	Lexington Historical Society, 2546
1817	"The Family Record 1817 Mary Russell's Work AE 13"	Embroidery	Location unknown
1818	"Eliza E. Parker 1818" (b. 1804) Age 14	Embroidery	Location unknown
ca. 1820	"Lucretia Bright" (b. 1807)	Embroidery	NSDAR
1820	"Family Record wrought by Elizabeth Stone 1820" (b. 1808)	Embroidery 16 x 15 3/4 in.	Huntington Library, Art Collections . . . Gail-Oxford Collection 2017.5.39
ca. 1805–1810	"The Family Record Faustina Mulliken's Work" (b. 1793)	Embroidery 17 x 15 in.	Location unknown
ca. 1805–1810 ?		Embroidery	Location unknown
ca. 1825	"Susan Garfield" (b. 1811)	Embroidery 20 1/2 x 16 in.	Private collection

	Father	Mother	Date of Marriage	Children	Location of Parents
62	Benjamin Howland (1770–1825)	Hephsibah Hastings (1770–1843)	3 June 1794	1795–1811	Dover
63	Samuel M. Bellows (1787–1821)	Mary W. Wyeth (1785–1860)	20 December 1808	1809–1816	Arlington
64	Josiah Mead (1761–1829)	Sally Locke (1766–1839)	12 May 1789	1790–1803	Lexington
65	Loah Locke (1783–1865)	Mary Foster (1784–1851)	15 March 1805	1805–1819	Lexington
66	Ebenezer Chenery (1765–1847)	Sally Hastings (1775–1866)	23 October 1803	1804–1820	Watertown/ Waltham
67	Thomas Ruggles Plympton (1782–1855)	Betsy Holden (b. 1787)	2 October 1805	1806–1828	Waltham ?
68	John Mulliken (1783–1855)	Susanna Reed (1784–1847)	30 November 1813	1814–1826	Concord/ Lexington
69	Jonathan Billings (1776–1841)	Rebeckah Hapgood (1780–1865)	24 April 1810	1813–1823	Acton

Embroidered Variants of the Middlesex County Type

	Father	Mother	Date of Marriage	Children	Location of Parents
70	Oliver Whitney (1786–1855)	Mercy Whitcomb (1791–1865)	16 March 1809	1811–1823	Harvard/ Lunenburg
71	Hezekiah Morse (1768–1854)	Sarah Bigelow (1771–1846)	30 May 1790	1791–1799	Weston/ Sherborn
71	Leonard Morse (1791–1849)	Clarissa Bartell (1792–1876)	29 April 1822	ca. 1825–ca. 1835	do.
72	John Rice (1768–1846)	Lucy Hubbard (1775–1851)	24 September 1797	1793–1806	Concord / Ashby
73	John Rice (1768–1846)	Lucy Hubbard (1775–1851)	do.	1793–1806	Concord / Ashby
74	David Carver (ca. 1740–1810)	Hannah Harlow (1742–1810)	ca. 1767	1768–1793	Taunton
75	Charles Holman (1788–1866)	Polly Converse (1791–1871)	25 July 1813	1815–1828	Bolton, Mass. / Marlborough, N.H.

Watercolor Variants of the Middlesex County Type

	Father	Mother	Date of Marriage	Children	Location of Parents
76	John Sterns [Stearns] (1765–1836)	Mary [Polly] Lane (1776–1815)	10 February 1800	1802–1815	Billerica
77	Thaddeus Brooks (1758–1819)	Sarah Winchester (1758–1835)	22 February 1785	1786–1803	Ashburn-ham, Mass.

Date of Record	Maker	Image Type / Dimensions	Owner/Dealer
ca. 1820–1825	"Wrought by Hephsibah Howl[and]" (b. 1809)	Embroidery	Private collection
1821	"Family Record wrought by Mary W. Bellows aet 11 1821"	Embroidery 15 3/4 x 19 1/2 in.	Stephen and Carol Huber
ca. 1812	"The Family Record Sally Mead's Work" (b. 1801)	Embroidery 15 x 12 in.	Huntington Library, Art Collections . . . Gail-Oxford Collection 2017.5.72
1825	"Lydia Locke, 1825" (b. 1813)	Embroidery	Private collection
1825	"Wrought by Lydia B. Chenery 1825" (b. 1812)	Embroidery 21 1/4 x 16 1/4 in.	M. Finkel & Daughter
ca. 1825–1829	"Family Record Louisa H. Plympton" (b. 1812)	Embroidery 15 1/4 x 16 in.	Private collection
ca. 1826	"Wrought by Susan Mulliken" (b. 1814)	Embroidery 22 x17 in.	Lexington Historical Society, 13228.1
1827	"Wrought by Sophia Billings aged 14"	Embroidery 17 1/2 x 16 3/4 in.	M. Finkel & Daughter

1825		Embroidery	Private collection
ca. 1809	"Sally Morse Ae 10 yr"	Embroidery	Location unknown
do.	do.	do.	do.
1811	Attributed to Lucy Rice	Embroidery	Location unknown
1814 ?	Attributed to Elmira Rice	Embroidery	Location unknown
1807–1810	Attributed to Ruth Carver	Embroidery	Campanelli Collection
1826 ?	"Wrought by Polly Holman" (b. 1815)	Embroidery 12 x 13 1/2 in.	Location unknown

ca. 1816–1820		Watercolor 15 1/2 x 12 5/8 in.	Ex collection Edith G. Halpert; location unknown
ca. 1814	"William Brooks" (b. 1803)	Watercolor 12 x 10 in. (sight)	Location unknown

	Father	Mother	Date of Marriage	Children	Location of Parents
78	Josiah Davis (1750–1815)	Abigail Hubbard (1754–1844)	October 1772	1773–1800	Concord / New Ipswich, N.H.
79	John Clement (1782–1867)	Hannah Pierce (1786–1847)	5 March 1805	1805–1824	Townsend
80	Eleazer Davis Jr. (b. 1768)	Martha Skinner (ca. 1775–1865)	1 January 1799	1799–1819	Bedford
81	Cyrus Wheeler (1798–1873)	Caroline August Wing (1803–1822)	29 November 1821	1822	East Montpelier, Vt.
81	Cyrus Wheeler (1798–1873)	Elmira Goodnow (1806–1884)	6 April 1828	1828–1848	do.

Calligraphers and Embroiderers Active in Townsend, Fitchburg, Ashby, and Sharon

	Father	Mother	Date of Marriage	Children	Location of Parents
82	Asa Farwell (b. 1768–1843)	Vashti Carter (1772–1853)	10 February 1796	1797–1810	Fitchburg
83	Adford [Adde] Jaquith (1785–1862)	Abigail Whiting (1786–1866)	3 July 1808	1809–1823	Ashby / New Ipswich, N.H.
84	Josiah Sawyer (1770–1800)	Patty [Martha] Wyman (1771–1845)	ca. 1794	1795–1800	Sharon, N.H.
84	Samuel Ryan (1771–1854)	Patty [Martha] Sawyer (1771–1845)	2 January 1803	1803–1816	New Ipswich, N.H.
85	John K. (b. 1769)	Olive K. (b. 1776)	1795		
86	Josiah Sawyer (1770–1800)	Patty [Martha] Wyman (1771–1845)	ca. 1794	1795–1800	Sharon, N.H.
86	Samuel Ryan (1771–1854)	Patty [Martha] Sawyer (1771–1845)	2 January 1803	1803–1816	New Ipswich, N.H.

"J. P." Types in Boston and Maine

	Father	Mother	Date of Marriage	Children	Location of Parents
87	Josiah Jones (1744–1787)	Susannah Bennett (d. Dublin, N.H. 1828)	22 November 1770	1771–1787	Lunenburg, Mass.
87	Samuel Lawrence (1737–1799)	Susannah Bennett Jones	20 November 1794	1796	Ashby, Mass.
88	Caleb Coolidge (b. 1753)	Rebecca Edwards (b. 1762)	10 March 1784	1785–1802	Boston / Machias, Me.

Date of Record	Maker	Image Type / Dimensions	Owner/Dealer
ca. 1810 to 1816		Watercolor	Location unknown
ca. 1825		Watercolor 18 x 16.75 in.	Rita King
1826	"Hannah S. Davis Bedford 1826"	Watercolor	Location unknown
after 1848		Watercolor	Location unknown
do.		Watercolor	Location unknown

ca. 1810		Watercolor	Ex collection Pam Boynton / Location unknown
ca. 1823		Watercolor	Private collection
ca. 1820–1825		Watercolor	Ex collection Edgar and Bernice Garbisch
do.		do.	do.
ca. 1825		Watercolor	Location unknown
ca. 1820–1825	"Wrought by Martha Ryan" (b. 1806)	Embroidery	M. Finkel & Daughter
do.	do.	do.	do.

after 1796		Watercolor 12 1/2 x 8 1/2 in.	Location unknown
do.		do.	do.
ca. 1815–1825	Attributed to J. P.	Watercolor 16 1/4 x 12 1/4 in.	Ex collection Mr. and Mrs. Jerome W. Blum

	Father	Mother	Date of Marriage	Children	Location of Parents
89	Samuel Matthews (1742–1788)	Abigail Chessley (1733–1811)	10 October 1762	1763–1784	"Georgies" (Castine?) Boston
90	Amos Pearson (1750–1784)	Marcy Sevey (1754–1807)	15 September 1772	1773–1784	Pownalborough, Me.

Pittsfield, N.H. (Odiorne and Others)

	Father	Mother	Date of Marriage	Children	Location of Parents
91	Enoch Blake Jr. (1796–1888)	Lydia Smith (1797–1875)	15 October 1818	1820–1823	Pittsfield, N.H.
92	Asa K [ ]	Sally Blake	15 February 1817		Pittsfield / Gilmanton, N.H. ?
93	Jonathan Connor (1765–1857)	Mary Allen (1765–1854)	14 February 1787	1788–1806	Gilmanton Ironworks, N.H.
94	Joseph Davis (1747–1803)	Hannah Akus (1755–1843)	10 July 1774	1795–1797	Newburyport, Mass.
95	Benjamin Sleeper (1779–1840)	Miriam Clough (1779–1861)	12 March 1806	1816	Gilmanton, N.H.
95	Samuel Gilman Kelley (1809–1884)	Amanda A. Sleeper (1816–1903)	23 October 1836	1838–1843	do.
95	Melvin W. Young (1835–1913)	Ellen G. Kelley (1838–1921)	27 November 1861		Pittsfield, N.H. ?
96	George Seavey (1768–1822)	Betsey Lane (1773–1849)	22 February 1796	1797–1811	Chichester, N.H.

Unclassified Rural and Urban

	Father	Mother	Date of Marriage	Children	Location of Parents
97	Joshua Cheever (1740–1813)	Abigail Eustes (1745–1809)	7 May 1765	1766–1790	Chelsea, Mass.
98	Nathan Holt (1725–1792)	Sarah Abbot (1730–1797)	4 August 1757	1758–	Andover, Mass.
99	Joshua Foss (1761–1831)	Elizabeth Hunt (1763–1849)	7 November 1785	1787–1801	Rye, N.H.
100	Ebenezer Spencer (1765–1851)	Mehetabel Buswel (1770–1855)	14 July 1791	1791–1805	Peacham, Vt.
101	Horace Janes (1789–1852)	Betsey Parker (1794–1856)	18 January 1816	1814–1834	Cornwall, Vt.
102	Daniel Winn (1741–1835)	Olive Berry (1748–1828)	11 January 1770	1772–1790	Wells, Me.
103	John McCurdy Smith Sr. (1759–1835)	Elizabeth McLelland (1764–1833)	17 September 1782	1783–1809	Buxton, Me.

Date of Record	Maker	Image Type / Dimensions	Owner/Dealer
ca. 1815–1825	"J.P." in lower right corner	Watercolor 30 cm x 24 cm	NEHGS Mss 1078
ca. 1815–1820	"J.P." in lower right corner	Watercolor 30 cm x 24 cm	NEHGS Mss 1075

ca. 1823	Attributed to Joseph Odiorne	Watercolor	Donald R. Randall
ca. 1825	do.	Watercolor	Peter H. Tillou collection
ca. 1810–1820	do.	Watercolor	Location unknown
ca. 1800	"Drawn by William Hodges"	Watercolor	Location unknown
ca. 1863–1865?		Watercolor	Historic New England, Beauport collection, 1942.2342.1AB
do.		do.	do.
do.		do.	do.
after 1811		Watercolor	Location unknown

"Decemr 30th 1799 (No 3)"	"by Edward Pratt Chelsea"	Watercolor 14 3/4 x 9 1/4 in.	Private collection
19th century		Watercolor	Location unknown
ca. 1820–1840		Watercolor	Location unknown
1805	"Record of the family of Ebenezer Spencer of Peacham County of caledonia and State of Vermont 1805"	Watercolor	U.S. National Archives
1831	"Lucretia Janes aet 11 Cornwall Vt"	Embroidery	Henry Sheldon Museum
ca. 1830		Watercolor 8 1/2 x 8 5/8 in.	Location unknown
1830	"By R. B. Smith, April 1830" [Royall Brewster Smith]	Watercolor (oil cloth)	Location unknown

Multiple Heart Images

	Father	Mother	Date of Marriage	Children	Location of Parents
104	Joseph Camp (b. 1744–1812)	Anna Kellogg (1749–1804)	5 December 1768	1770–1790	Newington, Conn.
105	Jeremiah Jolls (1750–1834)	Roby Salsbury (1747–1813)	30 December 1772	1774–1786	Stephentown (Albany) N.Y.
106	Benjamin Perkins (1767–1815)	Dorcas Stanwood (b. 1763)	11 October 1789	1791–1794	Newbury / Newbury-port, Mass.
107	Daniel Dodge (1745–1835)	Martha Moody (1739–1798)	18 November 1769	1770–1780	Newbury-port, Mass.
108	Daniel Dodge (1745–1835)	Martha Moody (1739–1798)	18 November 1769	1770–1780	do.
108	Daniel Dodge (1745–1835)	Mary Dudley (1746–1813) (Mary Kimball)	24 January 1799		do.
109	Joseph Stanwood (1761–1833)	Eunice Marchant (1763–1784)	19 January 1782	1783	Newbury, Mass.
109	Joseph Stanwood (1761–1833)	Sarah Dodge (1762–1810)	13 December 1785	1786–1801	do.
109	Joseph Stanwood (1761–1833)	Ruth Burnham (1769–1847)	5 December 1811		do.
110	Joseph Stanwood (1761–1833)	Eunice Marchant (1763–1784)	19 January 1782	1783	Newbury, Mass.
110	Joseph Stanwood (1761–1833)	Sarah Dodge (1762–1810)	13 December 1785	1786–1801	do.
110	Joseph Stanwood (1761–1833)	Ruth Burnham (1769–1847)	5 December 1811		do.

Suspect Documents

	Father	Mother	Date of Marriage	Children	Location of Parents
111	Job Parke (1790) (fictitious name)	Lucy Dey (1790) (fictitious name)	1811		
112	Rufus Meriam (1762–1847)	Martha Simonds (1766–1840)	23 August 1785	1787–1804	Lexington
113	Peleg Pinkham Jr. (1734–1810)	Jemima Chadwick (1736–1809)	4 May 1757 (alternate 18 March 1758)	1759–1770	Nantucket
114	[Blank tree with "tomato" blossoms]				

Date of Record	Maker	Image Type / Dimensions	Owner/Dealer
1787	"Made by Anna Camp in January AD 1787 &C" (b. 1773)	Watercolor 13 x 14 in.	Newington Historical Society and Trust Gift of the Camp family, 79-12:55
1806–1815	"Drawn by S. Morton" (Samuel Morton)	Watercolor 12.4 x 10.7 in.	Winterthur Museum, 1960.324.
1807	"Harriet Perkins Script"	Watercolor	Location unknown
1809	"Daniel M. Lankester Scrt. / Nov 4th 1809."	Watercolor	NEHGS
1809	"Daniel Moody Lankester, AE 14. Scripsit Novr. 13, 1809." "Newbury. East–School. B. H. Cheever"	Watercolor	NEHGS
do.	do.	do.	do.
1814	"Taken by Atkinson Stanwood Aet 13 / Feby 25th 1814"	Watercolor 14 3/4 x 12 in.	Museum of Old Newbury
do.	do.	do.	do.
do.	do.	do.	do.
1816	"Atkinson Stanwood, Newburyport, June 7 1816" (b. 1801)	Watercolor	Historic New England, 1992.464
do.	do.	do.	do.
do.	do.	do.	do.

20th century	"William Richardson"	Watercolor 19 3/4 x 13 3/4 in.	Location unknown
20th century	"Lexington, Mass. 1805 . . . by William Saville"	Watercolor	Location unknown
20th or 21st century	Nantucket, Mass., or Eastern U.S.	Watercolor	Location unknown
?		Watercolor	Location unknown

Appendix Sources

Sources are numbered to match the checklist items.

Nantucket Type

1 VR Nantucket 1:249, 343, 2:225, 249, 255, 5:325, 5:186, 190. Starbuck, *History of Nantucket*, 719. Gift of Grace Brown Gardner.

2 VR Nantucket 1:105, 2:27, 51, 78, 3:495; 5:296, 317. Gift of William F. Macy from the Estate of Lizzie Macy.

3 Nantucket VR 5:202, 281. Gift of Jane L. Folger.

4 Wheeler, *History of Stonington*, 323–324; *Barbour Collection*, "Copp" 3:234; Ehrlich, "Before Formal Education"; Watkins, "Smithsonian Previews"; Allen, *Family Record*, 8. Gift of John Brenton Copp.

5 Nantucket VR 2:137, 389, 475; 4:39, 5:351; Allen, *Family Record*, 9. Gift of Florence and Grace Bolles.

6 Nantucket Probate Records, 6:10; Nantucket VR 3:166.

7 Nantucket VR 2:597, 4:517. Carpenter and Carpenter, *Decorated Arts and Crafts of Nantucket*, 207. Mary Grace and Charles Carpenter to the author, 13 November 1986. Posted by Nina Hellman Antiques, 2348; January 2019.

8 Nantucket VR 1:176–182; 2:64; 3:178, 522; 5:105–106, 514. Gift of Mary C. Whippey.

9 Garth's Auctioneers and Appraisers, Columbus, Ohio: Sale 1045 Lot 685, 27 March 2010; Whitman, *Descendants of Stukely Wescott*, vol. 2, part 2, 56.

10 New Bedford VR 1:391–392; 2:449; Nantucket VR 2:339, 2:439; Jones, *Genealogy of the Rodman Family*, 71; communicated by Brian Ehrlich in 2015.

11 Nantucket VR 1:205, 5:208, 494; 5:295, 310; Carpenter and Carpenter, *Decorated Arts of Nantucket*, Plate LXV, 172.X4.

12 Image provided by NHA in 1987. Nantucket VR 4:400; 5:543, 547, 548; NHA Barney Genealogical Record.

13 Nantucket VR 5:250, 275. Gift of Jane L. Folger.

14 Prices4Antiques p4A Item D9791330, accessed May 2019; Nantucket VR 1:182–184; 3:182; 5:109.

15 Banks, *History of Martha's Vineyard*, 417; Edgartown VR 58, 166, 170, 257.

16 Nantucket VR 1: 466, 473, 499, 501, 504; 2:283, 444; Posted by Pook and Pook, Inc.; Prices4Antiques p4A Item F7985474, accessed May 2019.

17 Nantucket VR 2:339, 4:202, 226; 5:458. Gift of Mary L. Myrick Fuller.

18 Image provided by NHA; Nantucket VR 1:240, 288, 3:310, 449. Gift of Merwin Lodge.

19 Image provided by NHA; Nantucket VR 2:347; 4:246, 399; 5:468.

20 Nantucket VR 1:321; Prices4Antiques p4A Item E8954785, accessed December 2017; sold at Garth's Auctioneers and Appraisers, Lot 275, 25 November 2011.

21 Image provided by NHA; found in frame covering Gardner/Beard checklist number 2 (above). Gift of William F. Macy from the Estate of Lizzie Macy.

22   Image provided by NHA; lower part copies checklist number 18 (above). Gift of Merwin Lodge; Nantucket VR 3:279 (Coffin and Joy); Nantucket VR 4:369 (Simpson and Coffin); U.S. Federal Census for 1880 and 1900, Conn., Society of the Sons of the American Revolution: certificate by Edgar Riddell Thomas, cemetery inscription, Bridgeport, Conn., Nantucket VR 4:369 (Standish and Pollard).

Mass., N.H., and Maine Variants of Nantucket Type

23   Sinnett, *Richard Pinkham,* 241–242; Revolutionary War Pension and Bounty-Land-Warrant Application File R8260 NARA 300048.jpg.
24   Young, *Early Families of Sabattus* (under Thomas Alexander b. 1809); Prices4Antiques p4A Item E8848085, accessed September 2016; sold by Garth Auctions, 2015, Lot No. 623.

Saville, Pool, and Richardson in Gloucester

25   Gloucester VR 2:174, 177, 470; 3:266; Swan to the author, 16 December 1986.
26   Skinner Inc. American Furniture & Decorative Arts – 3278M Lot 395, 11 August 2019; Gloucester VR marriages (under Robbins) 460, births 587; (under Thurston) marriages 547; Ipswich VR births 314.
27   Shaffner & Klein, *Folk Hearts,* 56; *Kennedy Quarterly* 2 (January 1973): 6; Gloucester VR 1:409, 469; 2:328 (cited as P.R. 564).
28   Blanford & Blanford, *Beauport Impressions,* 53; Gloucester VR 1:508–527; 2:406.
29   Gloucester VR 1:420, 785; 2:593; 3:332 (cited as P.R. 592).
30   Little, *Little by Little,* 145; Ipswich VR 1:81; 2:73, 91, 398, 518; 3:510; Boulter, "Abraham Fitz–Hugh Channell"; Sons of American Revolution; Cleveland and Cleveland, *Genealogy of the Cleveland and Cleaveland Families,* 165–170, 340; Massachusetts VR: for Mary Dyer Smith Channell, November 19, December 6, 1807. Gift of Nina Fletcher and Bertram K. Little.
31   Blanford & Blanford, *Beauport Impressions,* 52, 53; Gloucester VR 1:308, 713; 2:249; 3:153 cited as P.R. 426.
32   John McInnis Auction, 26 August 2018; Gloucester VR 1:304.
33   *Kennedy Quarterly* 9, no. 3 (December 1969), entry 240; Gloucester VR 1:358, 526; 2:284; 3:172.
34   Swan, *Town on Sandy Bay,* 82–83; Marshall Swan to the author, 16 December 1986; Rockport VR 115; Gloucester VR 1:556, 668, 703; 2:510, 536; 3:305, cited as P.R. 903.
35   Gloucester VR 1:197, 290; 2:167, 236, 406, 413.
36   Gloucester VR 1:216, 306; 2:178, 245.
37   Sold by Kaminski Auctions, 29 October 2016, 4087. Gloucester VR 1:586; 2:460; 3:259.
38   Hollander, "Family Record," 313; Schaffner & Klein, *Folk Hearts,* 57; Rockport VR 47; Gloucester VR 1:151; 2:84; 3:70, cited as P.R. 174. Gift of Ralph Esmerian.
39   Gloucester VR 1:152; 2:187, 3:122; cited as P.R. 189; Marshall Swan to the author, 16 December 1986.
40   Gloucester VR 1:160–161, 709; 2:139, 537; 3:96; Marshall Swan to the author, 16 December 1986. Gift of Mrs. Frederick Tarr.
41   Brant & Cullman, *Small Folk,* entry 70; Gloucester VR 1:211, 294; 2:175, 239; 3:115 cited as P.R. 282.
42   Skinner catalogue, 2308, Lot 508 (19 February 2006); not cited in Gloucester VR.
43   Photograph courtesy of Gregory H. Laing (January 1996).

Middlesex County School[s] for Young Women

44   Waltham VR 91–92, 292; *Watertown Records* 5:120, 158; Bond, *Genealogies,* 1:605. Gift of Russell H. Kettell.
45   Billerica VR 185, 320; Bedford VR 102, 118; Sheila Rideout to author 1986; Van Wagenen, *Isaac Stearns,* 79; Bond, *Genealogies,* 1:467–471.
46   Locke, *Munroe Genealogy,* 8; Lexington VR 53–54, 190. Gift of Mrs. Jessie Allard Kline.
47   Garrett, "American Samplers," 688; Ring "Collecting," 90; Hudson, *History of Lexington* (1868), 255–256; (1913), 2:730–731; Bond, *Genealogies,* 1:12, 632.

48   Courtesy of Stephen and Carol Huber, www.AntiqueSamplers.com; Sotheby's, *The Joan Stephens Collection*; Clark, *Records*, 43–44, 74–75, 175–176.

49   Bolton and Coe, *American Samplers*, 113, 245; Garrett, "American Samplers," 230; Burlington VR 48–50; Woburn VR 1:291–292, 3:318; Sheila Rideout communication; Northeast Auctions, 3–5 August 2012.

50   Hudson, *History of Lexington* (1868), 140, 214; (1913) 2:431; Lexington VR 79, 187, 453.

51   Skinner catalog; Waltham VR 48, 49, 166, 204; courtesy of Stephen and Carol Huber, www.AntiqueSamplers.com.

52   Waltham VR 36–39, 345, 461; Bond, *Genealogies*, 1:241, 268; Swan, *Plain and Fancy*, 84. Gift of Mrs. Alfred C. Harrison.

53   Skinner catalog; Lexington VR 33, 91, 120, 179; Cutter, *Genealogical and Personal Memoirs*, 1426; Lucebia Windship was Anna Munroe Harrington's granddaughter.

54   Hudson, *History of Lexington* (1868), 151, 251; (1913) 2:715; Brown, *Copy of Epitaphs*, 161; Lexington VR 83, 156.

55   Nathan Russell under Ancestry.com; Lexington VR 70, 145, 467; Concord VR 219.

56   Bolton and Coe, *American Samplers*, 115, 204; Bolton and Coe, "Photographs"; Hudson, *History of Lexington* (1868), 173–174; (1913), 2:516-517; Parker, *John Parker*, 157.

57   Garrett, "American Samplers," 688–691; Watertown VR 3:153, 161, 188; Bond, *Genealogies*, 1:111–112, 214, Sebba, *Samplers*, 106; Allen, *Family Record*, 45.

58   Brown, *Copy of Epitaphs*; Nelson, "Collecting American Samplers"; Watertown VR 198, 233. Gift of Thomas H. Oxford and Victor Gail.

59   Matz and Pribell, *Hartman*, (1989), 256 and back cover; Lexington VR 50; Hudson, *History of Lexington* (1868), 142; (1913), 2:444.

60   Waltham VR 13, 113, 234; Bond, *Genealogies*, 1:16; listed: Prices4Antiques p4A Item D9783686, accessed May 2019; Mabel Mason, *Capt. Samuel Barnes . . .* ([Kingston, N.H.]: s.n., 1958), 6-9.

61   Waltham VR 41, 45, 155; Glee Krueger to the author 1982; 1987; Bond, *Genealogies*, 1:235, 268; Finkel and Daughter, *Samplings*, XXXIX (cover).

62   *Howland Quarterly* 32 (Jan.–Apr. 1968); Howland, *History*, 550.

63   Arlington VR (under Wythe) 49, 120.

64   Lexington VR 47, 131, 187; Hudson, *History of Lexington* (1868), 123, 135–136; (1913), 2:418. Gift of Thomas H. Oxford and Victor Gail.

65   Hudson, *History of Lexington* (1868), 125; (1913), 2:373; Lexington VR 42, 447; Judith Lund to author, 1982, 1986, 1987.

66   Finklel and Daughter, *Samplings* IV:3; Buckminster, *Hastings Memorial*, 71–72; Watertown VR 231.

67   Waltham VR 74, 305; Chase, *Plympton Genealogy*, (entry 79) 136; *NEHGS Register* 9 (1855); Schaffner and Klein, *Folk Hearts*, 30; Huber and Huber, "Catalogue Notes"; Sotheby's 4938, Lot 625.

68   Hudson, *History of Lexington* (1868), 143; (1913) 2:445–446; Lexington VR 50; Concord VR 370.

69   Acton VR 17, 18, 135, 175; Finkel and Daughter, *Samplings*, VI:9.

Embroidered Variants of the Middlesex County Type

70   Harvard VR 111–118, 232, *Maine Antique Digest*, June 1986, 16-A; Pierce, *John Whitney*, 102, 199; Sheila Rideout to the author, 1986.

71   Sherborn VR 68, 106, 214; Weston VR 129, 164, 167; Morse, *Genealogical Register*, 180; communications from Shiela Rideout, December 15, 1986, and Betty Ring 1986.

72   Bolton and Coe, *American Samplers*, 213–214; Concord VR 362; Bolton and Coe, "Photographs," vol. 3, P to S.

73   Bolton and Coe, *American Samplers*, 213–214; Concord VR 362.

74   National Soc. Col. Dames database, Family register #3764; *Family Tree Samplers,* online database; Campanelli and Campanelli, "Following the Threads."

75   Sold by Skinner 2006. Boston 2337, Lot 472.

Watercolor Variants of the Middlesex County Type

76 *Maine Antique Digest*, 7:5 (April 1979); Van Wagenen, *Isaac Stearns*, 185–187; Bond, *Genealogies*, 1:471; Halpert, *Folk Art Collection*, K369.

77 Stearns, *History of Ashburnham . . .*, 623; Crafts and Crafts, *The Craft Family . . .*, 137; Massachusetts, *Town and Vital Records, 1620–1988*.

78 Concord VR 207; *Memoirs of Members of the Social Circle in Concord*, 98–109; Chandler, *History of New Ipswich*, 313; posted on Antique Dealers Association accessed September 2017; later posted on Prices4Antiques P4A Item E8928683 accessed December 2017.

79 Posted by Antique Associates at West Townsend; Townsend VR 1:40 and 60, 252, 384, 360; Dracut VR 26.

80 Sold by Skinner June 14, 2018; Auction 311OT, Lot: 2005. Bedford VR, 18–20, 101.

81 Posted on Pricers4Antiques P4A Item C200822; Wheeler, *Genealogical and Encyclopedic History of the Wheeler Family*, 2:846, 1088.

Calligraphers and Embroiderers Active in Townsend, Fitchburg, Ashby, and Sharon

82 Fitchburg VR 2:244, 313–314, 3:159. Skinner auction 24 February 2015 2785T.

83 Ashby VR (births, 1809–1823; deaths 1810 to 1875).

84 Sotheby Parke Bernet, "Important Frakturs," *Garbisch Sale Catalog*, 12 November 1974.

85 Pam Boynton to the author, 30 October 1980.

86 Finkel and Daughter, *Samplings* XXXIV, cover, 1–2 (2008).

"J. P." Types in Boston and Maine

87 Pook and Pook, Inc., Downingtown, Pa., sold 21 April 2012, Lot 863; Massachusetts marriages in Ashby 1794, 27.

88 Coolidge family tree, Northeast Auctions, 14–16 August 2015; Bond, *Genealogies*, 2:747–748.

89 Image provided by NEHGS, R. Stanton Avery Special Collections; Find a Grave # 89049598 (George Matthews, d. 1877).

90 Image provided by NEHGS, R. Stanton Avery Special Collections; Find a Grave #151256938, 151237975, 89049601, 89049598; Allen, *History of Dresden, Maine*, 455; Pownalborough VR 16 January 1773.

Pittsfield, N.H. (Odiorne and Others)

91 *N.H., Marriage Records Index; N.H., Death and Burial Records Index*; Donald R. Randall to the author, 21 May 1989.

92 Tillou and Rovetti, *Nineteenth-Century Folk Painting: Our Spirited National Heritage,* no. 25.

93 Skinner catalog; ex collection Arthur and Sybil Kern; *US Federal Census, 1830*; Lancaster, *History of Gilmanton*, 55, 57; Arthur B. Kern to the author 19 March and 3 April 2002.

94 Garth's Auctions, Delaware, Ohio, 29 August 2003; *Lineage Book of the Charter Members of the DAR*, vol 44.

95 Clough Genealogy, *Descendants of John Clough*, 293; Kelly, *Descendants of John Kelly of Newbury*, 138; Sleeper Burial Ground, Gilmanton Iron Works, N.H.

96 *Maine Antique Digest,* Sept. 1987, says Drakes "were founding fathers of Pittsfield."

Unclassified Rural and Urban

97 Chelsea VR 64, 104, 360, 372, 413, 464, 521; Warwick Collection; Cheever's father was a member of the Artillery Co. of Boston.

98 Skinner sale 1608M Lot:1114 (2012).

99 Posted on eBay December 2016; *N.H., Marriage Records Index, 1637–1947*.

100 U.S. National Archives, Washington, D.C. RD-DC-1.

101 Matthews, *History of Cornwall*, 77–78; Janes, *The Janes Family: A Genealogy and Brief History . . .*, 213.

102 Skinner catalogue, 8 June 2003; sale #2198-1158. Ancestry.com; "Subject: John Winn (bapt. 1710-Maine)" posted 1997.

103 "Dan and Jan Olmstead Sell Their Collection at Auction," *Antiques and the Arts Weekly*, 30 September 2008.

Multiple Hearts Images

104 Benes, *Two Towns*, entry 284; Benes, *The Art of Family*, Fig. 11. Gift of the Camp family, 79-12:55.

105 Kern & Kern, "Painters of Record," 31.

106 Prices4Antiques p4A Item E8930916, accessed May 2019.

107 File photograph; Newbury VR 1:142; 2:144; Newburyport VR 1:233; 2:272.

108 File photograph; Newbury VR 1:142; 2:100, 144; Newburyport VR 1:233; 2:139, 272.

109 Newbury VR 2:460; Newburyport VR 1:361–363, 2:446–447, 793; Benes, *Old-Town and the Waterside*, entry 45; Benes, *The Art of Family*, Fig. 13; Allen, *Family Record*, entry 9.

110 File photograph; Selina Little to the author 29 and 31 March 1996; Newbury VR 2:460; Newburyport VR 1:361–363, 2:446–447; 793; Benes, *Old-Town and the Waterside*, entry 45.

Suspect Documents

111 Bishop, *Folk Painters of America*, 41; *Masterpieces of American Folk Art* (1975); formerly owned by the museum of IBM Corporation, New York City.

112 Photographed 1987 by Gregory H. Laing.

113 Posted online 2013. NHA Barney Genealogical Record.

114 Posted on Prices4Antiques.com, p4A Item E8954811, accessed May 2018.

Notes

1.   Noah Webster (1758–1843) retitled the *Grammatical Institute of the English Language* to *American Spelling Book* in 1788. It was the most popular American book of its time; Noah Webster, "Dissertation 1," *Dissertations on the English Language* . . . (Boston: 1789), 20.

2.   *New-England Palladium,* 6 May 1806. Williams's full quotation is: "Drawing of Family Records, neatly fil[l]ed up. He likewise teaches the polite art of Drawing, for young ladies and gentlemen. Those who cannot attend, may have lessons at their own houses." Williams's offer is the only known example advertising this service, though some publishers of Bibles (such as Mathew Carey of Philadelphia) provided four pages of "valuable Family Record . . . handsomely divided for marriages, births, deaths. &c." (*New London Bee,* 17 Feb. 1802.)

3.   Estate of Obed Marshall, Nantucket Probate Records Book No. 6, 1815–1824, p. 104. Katherine Walker and Marcy Grace and Charles Carpenter, all of Nantucket, kindly provided a copy of this entry.

4.   Ashley Bowen had been approached by his namesake Daniel Bowen who was raising money to replace the contents of the Columbian Museum in Boston, which had been destroyed by an accidental fire. William Bentley, *The Diary of William Bentley, D.D., Pastor of the East Church, Salem, Massachusetts,* vol. 3, 15 February 1809 (Reprint: Gloucester, Mass.: Peter Smith, 1962), 416: "He [Ashley Bowen] told me one of the name had been at Marblehead in a very beggerly way, alluding to Bowen of the Museum, asking his charity & that he gave him the tree of the Bowen family drawn by my pupil." The pupil is identified in an earlier Bentley diary entry (13 May 1807, 3:294–295): "[I] sent to Ashley Bowen, the worthy Companion of the Immortal Cook in 1759 at Quebec, the third drawing from the pen of my pupil H[annah] C[rowninshield]. The first was from a view of his life compared to the sailing of a Ship. The second was a tree of genealogy till the fourth generation, from the first Bowen who came to America." See also 5 May 1807, 3:293: "Sent to Ashley Bowen his Genealogical tree finished by my pupil to gratify that aged seaman entitled to notice for his venerable age & past services." The tree was published in 1973 as part of Ashley Bowen, *The Journals of Ashley Bowen (1728–1813) of Marblehead,* 2 vols., ed. Philip Chadwick Foster Smith (Boston: Colonial Society of Massachusetts, 1973), 2:613–614. (Plate XXXII, opposite 365, with genealogical and historical additions.)

5.   Bowered trees and chain genealogies provide the only other symbol types taught at young women's schools during this period. See Carol and Stephen Huber, "With Needle and Brush," catalogue essay describing genealogical samplers by Julia Ann Fitch (Metropolitan Museum of Art, 1807) and Sally Olcott Wells (Historic Deerfield, 1807) where a quiet garden scene is surrounded by a ring of touching circles containing the names of parents and children. Also see Peter Benes, "Decorated New England Family Registers, 1770 to 1850," in *The Art of Family: Genealogical Artifacts in New England,* ed. D. Brenton Simons and Peter Benes (Boston: NEHGS, 2002), 277–278, describing the activities of Mrs. Gill's Academy, West Cambridge, Mass.

6.   See, for example, Philip Zimmerman, "Reading the Signs: An Object History of Tavern Signs from Connecticut, 1750–1850," in *Lions and Eagles and Bulls: Early American Tavern and Inn Signs from the Connecticut Historical Society,* ed. Susan P. Schoelwer (Hartford: Connecticut Historical Society and Princeton University Press, 2000), 22–35.

7   See Appendix showing a checklist of 114 watercolor or embroidered genealogies using twin-heart and multiple-heart motifs. Previous lists were published in Peter Benes, "Decorated Family Records from Coastal Massachusetts, New Hampshire, and Connecticut," in *Families and Children: 1985 Annual Proceedings of the Dublin Seminar for New England Folklife* (Boston: Boston University Scholarly Publications, 1987), 94–146; Benes, "Decorated New England Family Registers, 1770 to 1850," 13–59, 275–282. Additional data have been gained from Gloria Seaman Allen, *Family Record: Genealogical Watercolors and Needlework* (Washington, D.C.: Daughters of the American Revolution, 1989) and from Donna Smith Fee, "Family Registers: Genealogical Decorative Art," *Historical Nantucket* 52, no. 2 (Spring 2003): 6–9. The majority of new family records were found on the internet as they changed ownership or were cited in pricing and storage archives. These sources are cited in the Appendix and Bibliography. There is, of course, a real disadvantage to relying on electronic sources because many websites are actually imperma-nent. In fact, some of the key items discussed here are no longer available online since the site has been closed down or is now restricted. And the same problem is true of privately owned pieces that are inaccessible to the public and those which are known only from photographs or second- or third-generation electronic images. Here, too, their reliability is questionable. Many new items, however, were transmitted by individuals or collectors. For example, one was communicated by a family that still owns the piece (Jaquith/Whiting [83]); two more (Cheev-er/Eustes [97], and Carver/Harlow [74]) were provided by collectors; two (Matthews/Chessley [89] and Pearson/Sevey [90]) are items held at the R. Stanton Avery Special Collections at the New England Historic Genealogical Society, which posted them on their website and kindly provided high-resolution images; and two more (Coffin/Folger [18] and Coffin/Folger [22]) by the Nantucket Historical Association, which also posted them on their website and sent the author additional high-resolution images.

8   Newbury, Massachusetts, gravestone of Henry Sewall, 1700, spelling modernized. Edward Taylor, "To the Family Relict," quoted in *The Puritans in America: A Narrative Anthology*, ed. Alan Heimert (Cambridge: Harvard University Press, 1985), 331, following the death of Samuel Hooker, minister at Farmington, Conn., 1697.

9   Woodbury/Lane family record, *Figure 5* [29]; "Sacred to the Memory of Betsy Dennison Daughter of William & Betsy Rowe," memorial tablet drawn by William Saville, 1793, Sandy Bay Historical Society. Taken from the second verse of Isaac Watts (1674–1748), "On the Sud-den Death of Mrs. Mary Peacock," Watts, *Horae lyricae: Poems* (London: Lawrence, 1706), Book II, 133, with the substitution of the word "Friend" or "Child" for "soul" in the first line.

10 Benes, "Decorated Family Records from Coastal Massachusetts, New Hampshire, and Con-necticut," in *Families and Children: 1985 Annual Proceedings of the Dublin Seminar for New England Folklife* (Boston: Boston University Scholarly Publications, 1987), 131–145; Benes, "Decorated New England Family Registers, 1770 to 1850," in *The Art of Family: Genealogical Artifacts in New England*, 275–282.

11 *The Whole Booke of Psalmes Faithfully Translated into English Metre* (Bay Psalm Book) (Cambridge, Mass., 1640), Psalm 1, verse 3.

12 An unfinished manuscript by Gutun Owain produced between 1488 and 1498, which contains texts about astrology, a calendar, a treatise on urine, the life of St. Martin, and genealogy and history from Adam to Asclobitotus. National Library of Wales, Aberystwyth, Mss 3026, p. 63.

13 "Typological life and genealogy of Edward IV (1460–ca. 1470)," miniature in colors, roll parch-ment, British Museum, Harley 7353.

14 "Typological life and genealogy of Edward IV (1460–ca. 1470)," miniature in colors, roll parch-ment, British Museum, Harley 7353.

15 "Biblical and genealogical chronicle from Adam and Eve to Edward VI," 1511, British Library, London, Kings Mss 395, fols. 32v–33r.

16 *Genealogical chart tracing the Tudor roots of Mary Stuart, Queen of Scots & her son James VI of Scotland & I of England,* English, 1603, oil on canvas, Parham Park, Nr. Pulborough, West Sussex, UK; Photograph by Mark Fiennes, the Bridgeman Art Library.

17   "The true portraiture of Geffrey Chaucer the famous English poet as by Thomas Occleve [Hoccleve] is described who lived in his time, and was his Scholar," taken from John Speed, *The Progenie of Geffrey Chaucer,* frontispiece in Thomas Speght, *The Workes of our antient and lerned English Poet, Geffrey Chaucer* (London: Adam Islip, 1598).

18   "Gentility," William Marshall (fl. 1617–1649), engraved title page, 3d ed. of Richard Brathwaite, *The English Gentleman and English Gentlewoman . . .* 1675 (London: John Dawson, 1641). Earlier editions under the title *The English Gentlewoman* were published in 1630 and 1631 using the same genealogical image produced by Marshall but showing the woman being courted by a prospective husband.

19   "Arbre généalogique de la Maison de Lorraine (France et Anjou)," 1505, Bibliothèque de l'Institut de France, Paris, manuscrits et imprimés, Mss 679, folio 80 verso.

20   "Genealogia divi beinrici imperatoris," illustration in Hartmann Schedel (1440-1514), *Nuremberg Chronicle,* Nuremberg, Germany, 1493.

21   Johann Michael Wilhelm von Prey, Collection on the Genealogy of Bavarian Nobility, vol. 27, Bavaria, 1724, online at World Digital Library, www.wdl.org.

22   "Stammbaum der Familie Bach, Ohrdrufer Linie," 1773, Staatsbibliothek zu Berlin – Preussischer Kulturbesitz.

23   The Antonio Joseph Cordero family tree is the property of the Daughters of the Republic of Texas Library, San Antonio. See Kelvin Meyers, "Investigating Your Family History," 31 August 2010, Daughters of the Republic of Texas Library.

24   Silver locket made for Samuel Moffat, Portsmouth, N.H., circa 1776, Museum of Fine Arts, Boston, accession number 40.751.

25   Posy, also spelled "poesy," was a one-line poem of endearment. See Joan Evans, *English Posies and Posy Rings* (London: Oxford University Press, 1931) index, 45, 46, 48, 108, 109, 119. For an American treatment of hearts see Cynthia V. A. Schaffner and Susan Klein, *Folk Hearts: A Celebration of the Heart Motif in American Folk Art* (New York: Knopf, 1984).

26   "LA'MOUR LES JOINT," French busk, seventeenth century, L. 13 5/8 in., Metropolitan Museum of Art, New York; accession 30.135.20; seventeenth-century busk (metal) given to Anne-Marie-Louise d'Orléans (1627–1693), Duchesse de Montpensier, Metropolitan Museum of Art, accession number 30.135.32.

27   Busk detail, wood, Strafford, Vt., 1782, gift of Aubigne L. Gergen, John A. Gergen, Kenneth J. Gergen, Stephen L. Gergen, and David R. Gergen, Winterthur Museum, Winterthur, Del., 1992.87. For additional information on Zachariah Brigden's silver box see Benes, "Decorated New England Family Registers," 24, fig. 10A.

28   Coffin coat of arms, Nantucket Historical Association Research Library, 1999.0053.002.

29   Phebe Folger Coleman, "Un Recueil: Containing Painting, Penmanship, Algebra and Pieces selected from various authors in prose and verse, with a few pieces in French with their translation / By Phebe Folger of Nantucket," 1797–1806, Houghton Library, Harvard University, MS Typ 245. For additional information about this manuscript see Natalie Panno, "'Ten thousand times ten thousand worlds': Phebe Folger's Recueil and the Transformation of Quaker Women's Culture in the Early American Republic," A.B. thesis (Harvard University, 2009).

30   "Two Roses," scrimshaw busk, whale skeletal bone, nineteenth century, New Bedford Whaling Museum, 1948.30.206, cited in Benes, "Decorated New England Family Registers," 51. The author thanks Judith Lund for bringing this item to his attention.

31   Heart-decorated busks, Nantucket Historical Association: for example, 1962.0069.001, 1987.0021.001, 1985.0135.020, and 1991.0340.001. Twin-heart images are also found on gravestones in Massachusetts. One marker in Rutland, Mass. (a northeastern suburb of Worcester), recorded the death of two family members in 1749: Micah and Abigail Moore, Rutland, Mass., who died 6 and 7 September 1749. Micah was seventeen years old; his sister Abigail was ten. Edward H. Duane, ed., *The Old Cemetery of Rutland, Worcester County, Mass.* (Rutland, Mass.: Rutland Historical Society, 1980), 18, whose source was *The Old Northwest Genealogical Quarterly* 5 (July 1902): 104.

32 See, for example, the illustrated family record found in John and Catharina Moyer (Meier), Revolutionary War Pension and Bounty-Land-Warrant Application R7532, Maryland (1797).

33 Castelo Branco Coverlet, illustrated in Cora Ginsburg, *Costume, Textiles, and Needlework,* 2008.

34 *Roiail Progenei of our Most Sacred King Iames . . .*, National Portrait Gallery, London, NPG D1370, npg.org.uk/collections; *Arbor coniugales Genealogica Iacob VI,* 1612, British Museum, accession 1849,0315.16; John Goddard, *The Tree of Mans Life,* 1639–1650, British Museum, accession 1847,0723.10, britishmuseum.org/collection.

35 An attribution to Phebe and Rebecca Folger is cited in Fee, "Family Registers," 6, but this is still conjectural; Michael R. Harrison to the author, 13 November 2017.

36 Eunice Gardner's father, Barnabas Gardner (1740–circa 1778), was the brother of Kezia Gardner (1733–1810), Abigail Paddack's mother. Eunice Gardner's uncle was Benjamin Cartwright. Eunice's mother, Abigail Cartwright Gardner (1742–1846), was the older sister of Benjamin Cartwright. Eunice apparently was not directly related to Peter Gardner. *The Barney Genealogical Record,* online database at NHA.org; online database at Ancestry.com. *Vital Records of Nantucket to the Year 1850,* 5 vols. (Boston: NEHGS, 1927), 5:83, 95, 105 (hereafter cited as "Nantucket, Mass., VR").

37 For the first Coffin/Folger [18], the date of 1831 is suggested by the death date of John Coffin. For the second Coffin/Folger [22], the date is suggested by the transcription on the reverse side reading "The balance was added by J. N. Standish, Jr., Oct – 1881," identifying John N. Standish Jr. and the October 1881 date.

38 The main evidence is that colors were applied hastily, leaving borders of flowers surrounded by uncolored paper; names were cut short; some missing letters were added afterwards.

39 For a recent study of this source, see Kathleen Staples, "Embroidered Evidence: Family Record Samplers in the Revolutionary War Pension Files of the National Archives, Washington, D.C." (paper given at "Embroidery: The Thread of History," Winterthur Museum, 20 October 2018).

40 U.S. Revolutionary War Pension and Bounty-Land-Warrant, Bridget and Thomas Pinkham, file R8260, Application Files, 1800–1900, Archive Publication Number: M 804, Archive Roll Number, 1938.

41 The father, Thomas Alexander, died in 1844 in Webster, Maine (*Libby Family Tree,* online at Ancestry.com). Thomas and Betsey Alexander's daughter Susan Alexander Libby (1815–28 May 1884) was buried in Sabattus, Maine (online at FindAGrave.com, Memorial #50407661, Susan Alexander Libby, accessed 12 December 2016). She was married in Cumberland, Maine (*Libby Family Tree,* online at Ancestry.com). In the 1850 and 1860 Federal Censuses, she and her husband Seth Libby were living with their five children in Wales, Maine (*United States Federal Census, 1850,* Wales, Kennebec, Maine, Roll 257, p. 51B; *United States Federal Census, 1860,* Wales, Androscoggin, Maine, p. 278, Family History Library Film 803432). Thomas and Betsey Alexander's son Horatio Nelson Alexander (born 18 May 1818), a mason and builder, was living in Boston, Mass., according to the 1870 Federal Census (*United States Federal Census, 1870,* Boston Ward 1, Suffolk, Massachusetts, Roll M593640, p. 192A, Family History Library Film 552139). Another son, Thomas Alexander (1809–1860) was born in Webster Plantation and died there 21 November 1860 (*Libby Family Tree,* online at Ancestry.com). Image of family record online at Prices4Antiques, p4A Item E8848085, accessed fall of 2016.

42 Saville background: Bentley, *Diary,* 14 May 1799, 2:306: "At Rollins' are found some infant specimens of Taste. Some monumental drawings in memory of some deceased Children, done by one Saville, a Schoolmaster, with such inscriptions as are adapted to the heart of a parent, & are the best tribute to the memory of the good we love." Additional Saville material is taken from *Vital Records of Gloucester, Massachusetts, to the End of the year 1849,* 3 vols. (Topsfield, Mass.: Topsfield Historical Society, 1917; Salem, Mass.: Essex Institute, 1923–24) (hereafter cited as "Gloucester, Mass., VR"), 1:643, 2:493; John J. Babson, *History of the Town of Gloucester, Cape Ann, Including the Town of Rockport* (Gloucester, Mass.: Procter Brothers, 1860), 284–285; and James R. Pringle, *History of the Town and City of Gloucester, Cape Ann, Massachusetts* (Gloucester, Mass.: privately printed, 1892), 92. See Saville's handwritten record, *SYA Family Tree,* Ancestry.com.

43 Saville married Esther Pool (born 1765), 1 March 1796. Pool's background: Gloucester, Mass., VR 1:552, 2:443, 3:247: born son of Mark and Anna, 14 October 1787; married Mrs. Anna Daniels, 21 December 1806; died 13 June 1838.

44 Richardson background: Gloucester, Mass., VR 1:577, citing Private Record 814.

45 Pringle, *History of the Town and City of Gloucester,* 92.

46 Four mourning watercolors signed by Saville are known. Besides the one honoring Hannah Gott (ex-collection Arthur B. and Sybil B. Kern, 1800), they include Betsy Dennison Rowe (Sandy Bay Historical Society, 1793); Abagail Channel (Historic New England, 1794); and Capt. Isaac Harding (location unknown, 1801). A fifth memorial was signed by Joshua Pool in 1819 and honored Solomon Robbards (location unknown).

47 Saville, "Plan of the green or training field in the Town Parish," 1823, Cape Ann Museum, Gloucester.

48 George Pendle, "Size Doesn't Matter at the Met," *The Daily Art, Exhibitions* (24 Feb. 2016), 1843magazine.com. In 1734, Buchinger made a similar tree for his own family; it recorded his own four marriages in 1701, 1706, 1720, and 1725 and the birth of fourteen children. He did not attach a coat of arms for himself and instead added a label identifying his wives below the image.

49 The transfer may have been the other way around, where Saville used the device first on a memento mori design and then incorporated it later into family trees images. Edith G. Halpert, *The Edith Gregor Halpert Folk Art Collection* (New York: Terry Dintenfass, [1970?]), K25; see also Philip M. Isaacson, *Vital Statistics: American Folk Drawings and Watercolors from a Private Collection* (Brunswick, Maine: Bowdoin College Museum of Art, 1986).

50 Saville, "Sacred to the Memory of Mrs. Abagail Channel," watercolor, Historic New England, Cogswell's Grant, gift of Bertram and Nina Little.

51 Of the 1,037 private records mentioned in the *Gloucester Vital Records,* published 1917 through 1924, eighteen were "family trees" and thirty-three were "family registers," the bulk of them owned in Rockport. Most were probably watercolors by either Saville or Pool.

52 See *Figures 60, 66, 67, 125,* and *127.*

53 The average age of girls completing embroidered family records in the Lexington-area school was about 13; the two youngest were 11, and the oldest was 18. See Appendix, checklist items 44–69, column Maker.

54 Levi B. Chase, *A Genealogy and Historical Notices of the Family of Plympton in America* (Hartford, Conn.: Plympton Manufacturing Co., 1884), entry 79.

55 Stephen and Carol Huber, "Catalogue Notes" accompanying sale of needlework samplers by Louisa H. Plympton, online at www.antiquesamplers.com, accessed spring 2017 (Plympton/Holden [67]). For similar treatment, see Underwood/Munroe [54], Mead/Locke [64], and Garfield/Hagar [61].

56 *Lexington, Mass. Record of Births, Marriages and Deaths to January 1, 1898* (Boston: Wright and Potter, 1898), 161 (hereafter cited as "Lexington, Mass., VR") (Thomas Winship and Anna Harrington, married 11 April 1793).

57 Lexington, Mass., VR 76, 156 (marriage of Polly and Jonas Smith, 26 March 1798).

58 Ethel S. Bolton and Eva J. Coe, *American Samplers* (1921; reprint, New York: Weathervane Books, 1973), 213–214. There is some confusion in this reference between Lucy Rice and her younger sister Elmira.

59 *Family Register* no. 3764, online database at National Society of Colonial Dames, nscd.org.

60 Dan Campanelli and Marty Campanelli, "Following the Threads of the Carver Fruit Tree Family Register," *American Ancestors* 13, no. 1 (Winter 2012): 20–25. Name of preceptress: Miss Sally Cady, "educated in the Capital." Samuel H. Emery, *History of Taunton, Massachusetts . . .* (Syracuse, N.Y.: D. Mason, and Co., 1893), 295.

61 Arthur B. Kern and Sybil B. Kern, "Painters of Record: William Murray and His School," *Clarion* 12, no. 1 (Winter 1986/1987): 31.

62 For samples of cultural movement in the Atlantic-based region, see Peter Benes, *For a Short Time Only: Itinerants and the Resurgence of Popular Culture in Early America* (Amherst: University of Massachusetts Press, 2016), chapters 14, 15, and 19.

63 Some embroidered look-alikes that are related to, but stylistically not part of, the taught curriculum of the Middlesex County group can be traced to Weston, Bolton, and Lunenburg. Among these are the Holman/Converse [75], Morse/Bigelow [71], and Whitney/Whitcomb [70] embroideries. None of these is associated with a school or known teacher. And sometimes these pieces introduce design characteristics of other embroiderers and calligraphers. In the embroidered family tree "Wrought by Polly Holman" around 1826 or 1828, Polly inserts blank death capsules next to each child born to her parents' 1813 marriage in Bolton, Mass. One of them is filled out, though the remaining five remain blank.

64 Avis Stearns Van Wagenen, *Genealogy and Memoirs of Isaac Stearns and His Descendants,* 2 vols. (Syracuse, N.Y.: Courier Printing, 1902), 1:186.

65 The Sterns/Lane watercolor [76] was owned by Edith Gregor Halpert, an early collector of folk art in New York City in the 1930s and 1940s and contributor to the Colonial Williamsburg collection; it was put on sale in the *Maine Antique Digest* 7, no. 3 (April 1979).

66 Children included Josiah, Abigail, Jonathan, Rebecca, Lucy, Thomas, Joel, Moses, Lucinda, Clarissa, George, Charles, Cyrus, and Cyrene. Charles H. Chandler, *The History of New Ipswich, New Hampshire, 1735–1914* (Fitchburg, Mass.: Sentinel, 1914), 313.

67 Ezra S. Stearns, *History of Ashburnham, Massachusetts* (Boston: Published by the Town by J. E. Farwell and Co., 1887), 900.

68 Stearns, *History of Ashburnham*, 901.

69 *Vital Records of Townsend, Massachusetts, to the end of the Year 1873* (Boston: NEHGS, 1992), 1:40, 60, 252, 360, 384; *Vital Records of Dracut, Massachusetts, to the Year 1850* (Boston: NEHGS, 1907), 26.

70 "A Record of the Births and Deaths of A. and M. Pearson and their Children," Mss 1075, "A Record of the Births & Deaths of S. & A. Matthews & their Children," Mss 1078, R. Stanton Avery Special Collections, NEHGS, Boston. In all likelihood "J. P." was James Patterson, of Pownalborough [1783–1828], who married Betsy Pearson, the youngest daughter on one of these registers and the only child whose death date is not shown. Amos Pearson's father, Jonathan Pearson (1713–1796), and his brother Jonathan (1754–1805) both died too early to be the J. P. artist. They were from Rowley and Ipswich, Mass.; Amos was born in Ipswich. Jonathan the father was born and died in Rowley (*Vital Records of Rowley, Massachusetts, to the End of the Year 1849* (Salem, Mass.: Essex Institute, 1928), 93, 155, 401, cited hereafter as "Rowley, Mass., VR"), and Jonathan the brother died in Newburyport, Mass. Amos and Mercy Sevey Pearson's youngest daughter, Betsy (20 July 1784–2 June 1871), married James Patterson (18 December 1783–25 November 1828) of Dresden, Maine, on 2 May 1812. Patterson genealogical data from Charles Edwin Allen, *History of Dresden, Maine: Formerly a Part of the Old Town of Pownalborough, from Its Earliest Settlement to the Year 1900* (Dresden, Maine: Twin City Printery, 1931), 455. Patterson was the son of William and Elizabeth Call Patterson, and all their children are listed on that page.

71 Derwood family tree; Goodwin Soper family tree, Ancestry.com; *Bangor Historical Magazine* (Bangor, Maine: J. W. Porter, 1885), 1:57, 59; *Columbian Centinel*, 5 June 1811, *US Newspaper Extractions from the Northeast, 1704–1930* [database online], Provo, Utah: Ancestry.com Operations, Inc., 2014.

72 A. E. Anton "Handfasting' in Scotland," *The Scottish Historical Review* 37, no. 124 (October 1958): 89–102.

73 Gloucester, Mass., VR 1:92.

74 *Genealogy of the Odiorne Family* . . . (Boston: Rand, Avery, and Co., 1875), 47.

75 "Peace be within thy walls & prosperity within thy palaces," Psalm 122:7, King James Version. Almira Larkin White, *Genealogy of the Ancestors and Descendants of John White,* 2 vols. (Haverhill, Mass.: Chase Brothers, Printers, 1900), 1:359, where he is described as "a farmer and teacher, known as 'Master Odiorne'; was town clerk at Pittsfield from 1802 to 1830 and his fine penmanship may be seen upon their old records." Harold E. Young, *History of Pittsfield, New Hampshire* (Pittsfield, N.H.: Town, 1953), 177–178.

76 Daniel Lancaster, *The History of Gilmanton* (Gilmanton. N.H.: A. Prescott, 1845), 55, 57.

77 Hannah Akus [Acors] was born on 14 October 1755 in South Hampton, Rockingham, N.H., daughter of Moses and Abigail [Acors]. Ancestry.com *New Hampshire, Birth and Christenings Index, 1714–1904* [Database online], Provo, Utah: Ancestry.com Operations, Inc., 2011.

78 Young, *History of Pittsfield,* 484–485. *Maine Antique Digest,* Sept. 1987, p. 22-A.

79 Brian S. Ehrlich, "Before Formal Education: The Homegrown Instruction of a Deaf Artist in Eighteenth-Century New England" (paper given at "Schooldays in New England, 1650–1900," Dublin Seminar for New England Folklife, Deerfield, Mass., 19–21 June 2015).

80 The first public school was founded on Nantucket in 1816. *Nantucket Gazette,* 6 May 1816.

81 *Vital Records of Newbury, Massachusetts,* 2 vols. (Salem, Mass.: Essex Institute, 1911), 2:100. The 1803 to 1811 Newbury, Mass., book of town payments includes four entries regarding Benjamin Hale Cheever's teaching: 7 October 1807, payment to "Master Cheever" for teaching the year at the north district in the first parish; his selection to teach at the Center school from 25 April to 14 May 1808; 11 December 1810, payment for the year teaching in the east district known as Joppa; 9 November 1811 payment for the year teaching in the north district in the first parish. He is referred to as "Instructor" in the announcement of his death published in the *Columbian Centinel* on 29 June 1822. Newbury *Town Payments and Town Poor.* Ancestry.com, Massachusetts, *Town and Vital Records, 1620–1988* [database online] (Provo, Utah: Ancestry.com Operations, Inc., 2011).

82 Zachariah G. Whitman, *The History of the Ancient and Honorable Artillery Company of Massachusetts (Revised and Enlarged), From Its Formation in 1637 and Charter in 1638, to the Present Time . . . ,* 2d ed. (Boston: John H. Eastburn, Printer, 1842), 286.

83 Peter and Leslie Warwick's email communication to the author, 20 March 2017. See *Vital Records of Chelsea, Massachusetts, to the Year 1850* (Boston: NEHGS, 1916), 360.

84 "Edward D. Burke's son fell overboard and was drowned out of Ship Harlequin, Wm. Clark Master, at Woolwich Bay." Quotation from Isaac Coffin, Nantucket judge of probate, 6 October 1796, kindly provided to the author in a letter dated 9 February 1987 from Barbara P. Andrews, Librarian, Nantucket Atheneum, citing files received from Judge Coffin, "A record of deaths from the earliest dates they can be collected since the Island of Nantucket was Inhabited by the Whites," under 1796, 10-6. The death of Burke's son, Edward D. Burke, is cited in the Nantucket, Mass., VR 5:99. Alexander Starbuck, *A Century of Free Masonry in Nantucket* (Nantucket, Mass.: NHA, 1903), 17.

85 Baltimore *Federal Gazette,* 12 April 1800. The Wood/Tupper family register (Appendix, checklist item 7) may place Burke in Nantucket in 1800 or 1802, however.

86 Daniel Stanton, a schoolteacher and presumably the calligrapher who worked on Nantucket, was reported missing from Portsmouth, R.I., on 30 June 1823 (*Nantucket Inquirer,* 26 Aug. 1823); see also *Rhode Island Republican,* 2 July 1823, which reported that Stanton had been missing about thirteen days.

87 A color image of this family tree was kindly given to the author by Gregory H. Laing.

88 Gregory H. Laing, personal communication, 1996.

89 Hudson, *History of the Town of Lexington, Middlesex County, Massachusetts* (Boston: Wiggin and Lunt, 1868), 370.

90 Abram E. Brown, *History of the Town of Bedford, Massachusetts* (Bedford, Mass.: privately printed, 1891), 19.

91 Miss Sprague / Elijah Stearns advertisement of a school in Bedford: Boston *Columbian Centinel,* 24 and 31 May 1806.

92 Warren Vincent Sprague, *Sprague Families in America* (Rutland, Vt.: Tuttle Co., 1913), 498; Phebe Fitch, death record, Ancestry.com. *Maine, Death Records, 1761–1922* [database online]. Provo, Utah: Ancestry.com Operations, Inc., 2010; FindAGrave Index 1600s–Current, Fitch Cemetery, Sebago Center, Cumberland County, Maine; Lee-Hard-Fitch-Lee family tree, Ancestry.com.

93 Many of these schools for young women housed boarding students, and often more students came from out of town than lived in the community.

94 Van Wagenen, *Genealogy and Memoirs of Isaac Stearns and His Descendants,* 46, 81, 189.

95 For earlier discussions of the Lexington-area teacher, see Benes (1985), "Decorated Family Records," 124n21, and Benes (2002), "Decorated New England Family Registers," 50n57.

96 Sources for women who may have run schools in Middlesex County 1800 to 1820: *Columbian Centinel,* 18 April 1794; 18 March 1807; 16 April 1802; communication from Judith N. Lund, 30 December 1986.

97 Hudson, *History of the Town of Lexington* (1913), 2:280, 456, 469, 715.

98 In Middlesex County: Mary Munroe [54], Anna Munroe [53], Nathan Munroe [46], Solomon Harrington [51], Daniel Harrington [53], Elizabeth Harrington [46], John Mulliken [59], John Mulliken [68].

99 Susanna [61] and Grace Hagar [52].

100 In Gloucester: David Lane [27], Deborah Lane [28], and Susanna Lane [29], James Parsons [35], Susanna Parsons [33], Sally Tarr [31], Lois Tarr [40]. In Nantucket: Eunice Folger [18], Rebecca Folger [13], Charles Folger [16], Alexander Folger [13], Eunice Folger [18, 22], and Walter Folger [3]; Ebenezer Gardner [2], Peter Gardner [8], Crispus Gardner [11], and Ebenezer Gardner Jr. [21].

101 A good example of an embroidered family register that was kept up to date is one "Wrought by Abigail Barnard of Pittsfield Mass. 1833," which included filled-out death dates for eight of nine children from 1804 to 1872. Cooper Hewitt, Smithsonian Design Museum, acc. no. 1941-69-19, gift of Eva Johnston, viewed online at www.alamy.com, image ID J9812J.

102 Nantucket, Mass., VR 4: 246. The genealogy identifies David Starbuck as a "widr., 67, gentleman."

103 Louise (George) Boulter, "Abraham Fitz-John Channell," in newsletter *Family Gatherings,* dated Jan. 1999, posted on FindAGrave.com, Memorial #134318243, Abraham Fitz-John Channell, accessed September 2017; *NEHGS Register* 13 (1859): 38.

104 *Records of Ipswich, Massachusetts, to the End of the Year 1849,* 2 vols. (Salem, Mass.: Essex Institute, 1910), 2:73, 91, 281, "Abraham Channel to Abigail Burnham both of Ipswich Dec. 9 1779." Record of annulment on 6 December 1809 in *Boston Marriage Publications, 1807–1817,* vol. 8, Ancestry.com, Massachusetts, Town and Vital Records, 1620–1988 [database online] (Provo, Utah: Ancestry.com Operations, Inc., 2011); Boulter, "Abraham Fitz-John Channell"; Sons of the American Revolution, application file for Charles Stewart Channell, 9 January 1858, "son of Abraham Fitz John Channell [and] Welthy Cox." The evidence suggests some discrepancy about Abraham's age: Saville's family record says born 1759, not 1748 as cited in his obituary. Other examples of erasures include the maiden name of Daniel Dodge's second wife (Mary Dudley) from a record executed by his grandson (Daniel Moody Lankester) and changed to her married name (Kimball) at the time of her marriage to Dodge in 1799 (Dodge/Moody [108]).

105 Susan Jaquith email communication to the author, 16 October 2014.

106 Copp: Object file, National Museum of American History, Smithsonian, ID number DL.006820. Nantucket descendant quotation comes from J. N. Standish's inscription on the back of Coffin/Folger [22]: "The reverse of this, that is, the first three circles is a copy of an old family record executed over one hundred years ago, and for many years hung over the fire place at the old homestead in Nantucket Mass." Other examples: Joseph Spencer of Peacham, Vt., son of Ebenezer Spencer and Mehitabel Buswel Spencer, testified on 2 October 1851 for his mother's pension application: "I further Say that the paper hereto annexed is the original family record of the marriage of my father & mother and of the births of their children, and has existed in the family ever Since my earliest recollection." Ebenezer Spencer, N.H., Revolutionary War Pension and Bounty-Land-Warrant Application File W19392.

107 Noah Webster, *The American Spelling Book* (Hartford: Hudson and Goodwin, 1787); Webster, *The American Spelling Book,* rev. impression (Hartford: Hudson and Goodwin, 1809), 82. The Webster text reads: "Art thou a son or a daughter? Be grateful to thy father, for he gave thee life: and to thy mother, for she sustained thee."

108 D. Fenning, *A New Grammar of the English Language* (London: S. Crowder, 1787), 130.

109 Fenning, *A New Grammar of the English Language,* 105; Charles N. Sinnett, *Richard Pinkham of Old Dover, New Hampshire, and His Descendants* (Concord, N.H.: Rumford Printing, 1908), 241.

110 Psalm 122:7, King James Version.

111 This same couplet is found on a sampler exhibited at the historical society in Litchfield, Connecticut, 1909, which was worked by eleven-year-old Harriet Woods, showing "a large apple tree, on which . . . are embroidered the name and date of birth of each ancestor . . . and two hearts entwined" with her father's and mother's name, and the date of their marriage. Jeanie Gould Lincoln, "The Historic Homes of Litchfield," Part 1, *House and Garden* 16 (1909): 56.

112 Inscription fragments include: "Peace be within thy walls & prosperity within thy palaces" [91, 93, 95]; "Keep sacred the memory of your Ancestors" [89, 90]; "and have issue" [107, 108]; "taken by" [109]; "stillborn" [77]; "a child . . . died" [29]; "he died" [24, 83, 89]; "she died" [83, 89]; "died at Milton" [23]; "departed this life" [105]; "unto whom was born" [23]; "was drowned" [35]; "lost at sea" [8]; "A Record of the Births and Deaths of . . . ." [87, 88, 89, 90]; "They were united in marriage" [25] and most other Gloucester registers.

113 Because Bridget Pinkham was unable to prove her husband's war service, her claim was denied. Thomas Pinkham, N.H., U.S. National Archives, Revolutionary War Pension and Bounty-Land-Warrant Application File R8260.

114 Ebenezer Spencer, N.H., Revolutionary War Pension and Bounty-Land-Warrant Application File W19392.

115 Benes, *For a Short Time Only*, 345–349.

116 John Jenkins, Mass., Revolutionary War and Bounty-Land-Warrant Application File R5568; Allen, *Family Record: Genealogical Watercolors and Needlework*, 25.

117 Aimee E. Newell, *A Stitch in Time: The Needlework of Aging Women in Antebellum America* (Athens: Ohio University Press, 2014), 153–156.

118 From the reverse of Coffin/Folger [22] (see note 37 above). Standish may have signed his work: "The balance was added by J. N. Standish, Jr., Oct — 1881."

119 Nantucket Historical Association Research Library accession data, 2003.23.6 and 2003.23.5, both gifts of Merwin Lodge, a descendant of J. N. Standish, Jr. The author thanks the Nantucket Historical Association for posting the unusual Coffin/Folger genealogies on its website (www. nha.org) and for providing relevant genealogical data and additional images.

120 *1880 U.S. Federal Census*, Bridgeport, Fairfield, Connecticut, Roll: 95, page: 527B, enumeration district 131, online at Ancestry.com. A related example is the Sleeper/Clough [95] piece where the original was done for a marriage in 1806, but the presumed copyist included a member killed in the Civil War battle at Chancellorsville, Va., in 1863.

121 Robert Bishop, *Folk Painters of America* (New York: E. P. Dutton, 1979), 41; Sandra Brant and Elissa Cullman, *Small Folk: A Celebration of Childhood in America* (New York: E. P. Dutton, 1980), 54; *Masterpieces of American Folk Art,* September 30–November 29th, 1975, John Gordon, guest curator, Monmouth Museum, Lincroft, N.J. John Gordon's papers, including those that housed the 1975 exhibition, are kept at the archives of the American Folk Art Museum. See "A Guide to the John Gordon Papers A0020," article online at www.folkartmuseum.libraryhost.com.

122 Photographed by Gregory H. Laing in Byfield, Mass., 1987, in company with the author. For the sale of this item, see citation by WorthPoint.com in 2007.

123 "18th Century Nantucket Pinkham & Chadwick Family Tree Watercolor and Ink on Paper," posted 12 Oct. 2013 online at rafaelosonaauction.com.

124 Bentley, *Diary,* 14 and 15 May 1799, 2:306, 308; n42 above.

125 Van Wagenen, *Genealogy and Memoirs of Isaac Stearns and His Descendants,* 1:186. This is the full quotation: "John Stearns, born 1765, built the present Stearns homestead and established a home on one quarter of the farm, where his grandson was a late owner. Among many treasured relics is a rude picture, representing the family-tree, with a heart-shaped apple to record each birth in the family of John and Mary (Lane) Stearns, married Feb. 10, 1800, according to this record. The first fruit, on this family tree was Franklin Stearns, b. 1802, who spent his life of four score years on this farm, with a faithful wife, who laughingly boasted 'I was born in the year one.' 1801. She was the last of thirteen children of Benjamin Lane, who lived near the Stearns settlement."

126 For the efforts of Americans to re-Europeanize their culture, see Benes, *For a Short Time Only,* 20, 23, 32, 204, 233, 306, 374.

127 J. Hector St. John de Crèvecœur, *Letters from Nantucket and Martha's Vineyard* (Boston: Applewood Books, 1986), 72.

128 Labov, *Sociolinguistic Patterns* (Philadelphia: University of Pennsylvania Press, 1972), 6–7.

129 Beatrix Rumford, *American Folk Portraits from the Abby Aldrich Folk Art Center* . . . (Boston: New York Graphic Society; Williamsburg, Va.: Colonial Williamsburg Foundation, 1981); Deborah M. Child, *Soldier Engraver Forger: Richard Brunton's Life on the Fringe in America's New Republic* (Boston: NEHGS, 2015); Rufus Porter Museum, "Family Register of Jabez Amsbury and Nancy Miller," ca. 1822, cited in Laura Fecych Sprague and Justin Wolff, eds., *Rufus Porter's Curious World: Art and Invention in America, 1815–1860* (University Park, Pa.: Penn State University Press, 2019). See "A Family Genealogy Samuel Beals and Rebekah Wilkerson," Boston, 1795 (online at www.williamreesecompany.com, Bulletin 46: Manuscripts). Cardozo's interesting genealogy was kindly provided by Georgia B. Barnhill.

130 Kern and Kern, "Painters of Record," 28–35; Kern and Kern, "Almira Edson, Painter of Family Registers," *Magazine Antiques* 122, no. 3 (September 1982): 558–561.

Bibliography

Acton, Mass., VR: *Vital Records of Acton, Massachusetts, to the Year 1850.* Boston: NEHGS, 1923.

Allen, Charles Edwin. *History of Dresden, Maine: Formerly a Part of the Old Town of Pownalborough, from Its Earliest Settlement to the Year 1900.* Dresden, Maine: Twin City Printery, 1931.

Allen, Gloria Seaman. *Family Record: Genealogical Watercolors and Needlework.* Washington, D.C.: Daughters of the American Revolution, 1989.

Arlington, Mass., VR: *Vital Records of Arlington, Massachusetts, to the year 1850.* Boston: NEHGS, 1904.

Ashburnham, Mass., VR: *Vital Records of Ashburnham, Mass., to the end of the year 1849.* Worcester, Mass.: Rice, 1909.

Ashby, Mass., VR: "Town and Vital Records, 1756–1863. Ashby, Massachusetts, Town Clerk." Filmed by the Genealogical Society of Utah, 1971. Digitized by FamilySearch International, 2012. Viewed online at Massachusetts, Town Clerk, Vital and Town Records, 1626–2001. https://FamilySearch.org.

Babson, John J. *History of the Town of Gloucester, Cape Ann, Including the Town of Rockport.* Gloucester, Mass.: Procter Brothers, 1860.

Banks, Charles Edward. *History of Martha's Vineyard, Dukes County, Massachusetts.* 3 vols. Edgartown, Mass.: Dukes County Historical Society, 1966.

The Barbour Collection of Connecticut Town Vital Records. Edited by Lorraine C. White. Baltimore, Md.: Genealogical Publishing Co., 1984–2002.

Bedford, Mass., VR: *Vital Records of Bedford, Massachusetts, to the year 1850.* Boston: NEHGS, 1903.

Benes, Peter. *Two Towns, Concord and Wethersfield: A Comparative Exhibition of Regional Culture, 1635–1850.* Concord, Mass.: Concord Antiquarian Society, 1982.

Benes, Peter. *Old-Town and the Waterside: Two Hundred Years of Tradition and Change in Newbury, Newburyport, and West Newbury, 1635–1835.* Newburyport, Mass.: Historical Society of Old Newbury, 1986.

Benes, Peter. "Decorated Family Records from Coastal Massachusetts, New Hampshire, and Connecticut." In *Families and Children: 1985 Annual Proceedings of the Dublin Seminar for New England Folklife.* Boston: Boston University Scholarly Publications, 1987.

Benes, Peter. "Decorated New England Family Registers, 1770 to 1850." In *The Art of Family: Genealogical Artifacts in New England*, edited by D. Brenton Simons and Peter Benes. Boston: NEHGS, 2002.

Benes, Peter. *For a Short Time Only: Itinerants and the Resurgence of Popular Culture in Early America.* Amherst: University of Massachusetts Press, 2016.

Benes, Peter. "'Art Thou a Son? Or a Daugter?': Compelling New Evidence on Decorated Family Trees in New England, 1770–1850." Presented at the Deerfield-Wellesley Symposium, Deerfield, Mass., 18 March 2017.

Bentley, William. *The Diary of William Bentley, D.D., Pastor of the East Church, Salem, Massachusetts.* 4 vols. 1905–1914. Reprint, Gloucester, Mass.: Peter Smith, 1962.

Billerica, Mass., VR: *Vital Records of Billerica, Massachusetts, to the year 1850.* Boston: NEHGS, 1908.

Bishop, Robert. *Folk Painters of America.* New York: E. P. Dutton, 1979.

Blanford, William K., and Elizabeth C. Blanford. *Beauport Impressions: An Introduction to Its Collections.* Boston: SPNEA, 1965.

Bolton, Ethel S., and Eva J. Coe. *American Samplers.* 1921. Reprint, New York: Weathervane Books, 1973.

Bolton, Ethel S., and Eva J. Coe. "Photographs collected during the preparation of 'American Samplers,'" 1914–1918. 4 vols. Massachusetts Society of the Colonial Dames of America, 1921. Worcester Art Museum, Worcester, Mass. Available online at nscda.org.

Bond, Henry. *Genealogies of the Families and Descendants of the Early Settlers of Watertown, Mass., Waltham and Weston.* 2 vols. in 1. Boston: NEHGS, 1860.

Boston Marriage Publications, 1807–1817, vol. 8. Ancestry.com, Massachusetts, Town and Vital Records, 1620–1988 [database online] (Provo, Utah: Ancestry.com Operations, Inc., 2011).

Boston, Massachusetts, Marriages, 1700–1809. Online database, Ancestry.com, 2000.

Boston, Massachusetts, Registry Department. *Boston Marriages from 1700 to 1751.* Vol. 1. Boston, Mass.: Municipal Print, 1898.

Boston, Massachusetts, Registry Department. *Boston Marriages from 1752 to 1809.* Vol. 2. Boston, Mass.: Municipal Print, 1903.

Boulter, Louise George. "Abraham Fitz-John Channell." Text of the newsletter *Family Gatherings*, dated January 1999. Posted on FindAGrave.com, Memorial #134318243, Abraham Fitz-John Channell, accessed September 2017.

Bowen, Ashley. *The Journals of Ashley Bowen (1728–1813) of Marblehead.* Edited by Chadwick Foster Smith. 2 vols. Boston: Colonial Society of Massachusetts, 1973.

Brant, Sandra, and Elissa Cullman. *Small Folk: A Celebration of Childhood in America.* New York: E. P. Dutton, 1980.

Brathwaite, Richard. *The English Gentleman and English Gentlewoman . . . .* London: Printed by John Dawson, 1641.

Brown, Abram E. *History of the Town of Bedford, Massachusetts.* Bedford, Mass.: privately printed, 1891.

Brown, Francis H. *A Copy of Epitaphs in the Old Burying-Grounds of Lexington, Massachusetts.* Lexington, Mass: Historical Society, 1905.

Buckminster, Lydia N. H. *The Hastings Memorial: A Genealogical Account of the Descendants of Thomas Hastings.* Boston: Samuel G. Drake, 1866.

Burlington VR: *Vital Records of Burlington, Massachusetts, to the Year 1850.* Boston: NEHGS, 1915.

Campanelli, Dan, and Marty Campanelli. "Following the Threads of the Carver Fruit Tree Family Register." *American Ancestors* 13, no. 1 (Winter 2012): 20–25.

Carlisle, Mass., VR: *Vital Records of Carlisle, Massachusetts, to the End of the Year 1849.* Salem, Mass.: Essex Institute, 1918.

Carpenter, Charles H., and Mary G. Carpenter. *The Decorative Arts and Crafts of Nantucket.* New York: Dodd, Mead, 1987.

Chandler, Charles H. *The History of New Ipswich, New Hampshire, 1735–1914.* Fitchburg, Mass.: Sentinel, 1914.

Chase, Levi B. *A Genealogy and Historical Notices of the Family of Plympton in America.* Hartford, Conn.: Plympton Manufacturing Co., 1884.

Chelsea, Mass., VR: *Vital Records of Chelsea, Massachusetts, to the Year 1850.* Boston: NEHGS, 1916.

Child, Deborah M. *Soldier, Engraver, Forger: Richard Brunton's Life on the Fringe in America's New Republic.* Boston: NEHGS, 2015.

Clark, John. *Records of the Descendants of Hugh Clark of Watertown, Mass., 1640–1866.* Boston: privately printed, 1866.

Cleveland, Edmund J., and Horace G. Cleveland. *The Genealogy of Cleveland and Cleaveland Families.* Hartford, Conn.: Case, Lockwood and Brainard, 1899.

Clough Genealogy: A Genealogy of the Descendants of John Clough of Salisbury, Massachusetts. Bethel, Maine: John Clough Genealogical Society, 1952–1966.

Compiled Marriages, 1633–1850. Online database, Ancestry.com, 2005.

Concord, Mass., VR: *Concord, Massachusetts, Births, Marriages, and Deaths 1635–1850.* Concord, Mass.: Printed by the Town, 1895.

Connecticut, Deaths and Burials Index, 1650–1934. Online database, Ancestry.com, 2011.

Connecticut Town Birth Records, pre-1870 (Barbour Collection). Online database, Ancestry.com, 2006.

Connecticut, Wills and Probate Records, 1609–1999. Online database, Ancestry.com, 2015.

Crafts, James M., and William F. Crafts. *The Crafts Family: A Genealogical and Biographical History. . . .* Northampton, Mass.: Gazette Printing Company, 1893.

Crèvecœur, J. Hector St. John de. *Letters from Nantucket and Martha's Vineyard.* Boston: Applewood Books, 1986.

Cutter, William R. *Genealogical and Personal Memoirs.* New York: Lewis Historical Publishing, 1908.

Dracut, Mass., VR: *Vital Records of Dracut, Massachusetts, to the Year 1850.* Boston: NEHGS, 1907.

Duane, Edward H., ed. *The Old Cemetery of Rutland, Worcester County, Mass.* Rutland, Mass.: Rutland Historical Society, 1980.

Edgartown, Mass., VR: *Vital Records of Edgartown, Massachusetts, to the Year 1850.* Boston: NEHGS, 1906.

Edmonds, Mary Jaene. *Samplers and Samplermakers: An American School Girl Art, 1700–1850.* New York: Los Angeles County Museum of Art, 1991, 64–67.

Ehrlich, Brian S. "Before Formal Education: The Homegrown Instruction of a Deaf Artist in Eighteenth-Century New England." Paper given at "Schooldays in New England, 1650–1900," at the Dublin Seminar for New England Folklife. Deerfield Mass., 19–21 June 2015.

Emery, Samuel H. *History of Taunton, Massachusetts . . . .* Syracuse, N.Y.: D. Mason, and Co., 1893.

Evans, Joan. *English Posies and Posy Rings.* London: Oxford University Press, 1931.

Fee, Donna Smith. "Family Registers: Genealogical Decorative Art." *Historical Nantucket* 52, no. 2 (Spring 2003): 6–9.

Fenning, D. *A New Grammar of the English Language.* London: S. Crowder, 1787. Available also in Joseph F. Winks, *Choice Pieces, from British and American Authors.* London: G. Wightman; Leicester: Printed and sold by J. F. Winks, [1830?].

Finkel, M. and Daughter. *Samplings.* Philadelphia: privately printed, IV (1993), VI (1994), XXXIV (2008), XXXIX (2011).

Garrett, Elizabeth D. "American Samplers and Needlework Pictures in the DAR Museum. Part II: 1806–1840." *Magazine Antiques* 107, no. 4 (April 1975): 688–701.

Genealogy of the Odiorne Family . . . . Boston: Rand, Avery, and Co., 1875.

Gloucester, Mass., VR: *Vital Records of Gloucester, Massachusetts, to the End of the year 1849.* 3 vols. Topsfield, Mass.: Topsfield Historical Society, 1917; Salem, Mass.: Essex Institute, 1923–24.

Halpert, Edith G. *The Edith Gregor Halpert Folk Art Collection.* New York: Terry Dintenfass, [1970?].

Harvard, Mass., VR. Baldwin, Thomas Williams. *Vital Records of Harvard, Massachusetts, to the Year 1850.* Boston: [Wright and Potter Print Co.], 1917.

Hollander, Stacy C. "Family Record for Andrew Bickford and Olive Clark." In *American Anthem: Masterworks from the American Folk Art Museum,* 313. New York: Harry Abrams in association with American Folk Art Museum, 2001.

Howland, Franklyn. *A Brief Chronological and History.* New Bedford, Mass.: privately printed, 1885.

Huber, Steven, and Carol Huber. "Catalogue Notes": text accompanying sale of needlework samplers by Louisa H. Plympton. Viewed online at www.antiquesamplers.com, accessed spring 2017.

Huber, Steven, and Carol Huber. "With Needle and Brush: Schoolgirl Embroidery from the Connecticut River Valley, 1740–1840." In *With Needle and Brush: Schoolgirl Embroidery from the Connecticut River Valley, 1740–1840,* edited by Carol and Stephen Huber, Susan P. Schoelwer, and Amy Kurtz Lansing, 3–19. Old Lyme, Conn.: Florence Griswold Museum; Middletown, Conn.: published in association with Wesleyan University Press, 2011.

Hudson, Charles. *History of the Town of Lexington, Middlesex County, Massachusetts.* Boston: Wiggin and Lunt, 1868.

Hudson, Charles. *History of the Town of Lexington, Middlesex County.* 2 vols. Boston and New York: Houghton and Mifflin, 1913.

"Important Frakturs, Embroidered Pictures, Theorem Paintings, Cutwork Pictures and Other American Folk Art from the Collection of Edgar William and Bernice Chrysler Garbisch. Part III." New York: Sotheby Parke Bernet, 1974.

Ipswich, Mass., VR: *Records of Ipswich, Massachusetts, to the End of the Year 1849.* 2 vols. Salem, Mass.: Essex Institute, 1910.

Isaacson, Philip M. *Vital Statistics: American Folk Drawings and Watercolors from a Private Collection.* Brunswick, Maine: Bowdoin College Museum of Art, 1986.

Janes, Frederic. *The Janes Family: A Genealogy and Brief History of the Descendants of William Janes the Emigrant Ancestor of 1637 . . . .* New York: John H. Digman, 1868.

Jay, Ricky. *Matthias Buchinger: "The Greatest German Living."* Los Angeles, Calif.: Siglio, 2016.

Jones, Charles H. *Genealogy of the Rodman Family.* Philadelphia, Pa.: Allen, Lane, and Scott, 1886.

Kelly, Giles M. *Genealogical Account of the Descendants of John Kelly of Newbury, Massachusetts.* Albany, N.Y.: Munsell, 1868.

Kern, Arthur B., and Sybil B. Kern. "Almira Edson, Painter of Family Registers." *Magazine Antiques* 122, no. 3 (September 1982): 558–561.

Kern, Arthur B., and Sybil B. Kern. "Painters of Record: William Murray and His School." *Clarion* 12, no. 1 (Winter 1986/1987): 28–35.

Labov, William. *Sociolinguistic Patterns.* Philadelphia: University of Pennsylvania Press, 1972.

Lancaster, Daniel. *The History of Gilmanton.* Gilmanton, N.H.: A. Prescott, 1845.

Lexington, Mass., VR: *Lexington, Mass. Record of Births, Marriages and Deaths to January 1, 1898.* Boston: Wright and Potter, 1898.

Lineage Book of the Charter Members of the DAR [1895–1921]. 166 vols. Washington, D.C.: DAR, 1891.

Little, Nina F. *Little by Little: Six Decades of Collecting American Decorative Arts.* Hanover, N.H.: SPNEA, 1998.

Locke, John D. *The Munroe Genealogy.* Boston: J. Munroe and Co., 1853.

Massachusetts Compiled Birth, Marriage, and Death Records, 1700–1850. Online database, Ancestry.com, 2018.

Massachusetts VR: *Massachusetts, Town and Vital Records, 1620–1988.* Online database, Ancestry.com, 2011.

Masterpieces of American Folk Art. September 30–November 29th, 1975. John Gordon, guest curator. Lincroft, N.J.: Monmouth Museum, 1975.

Matthews, Lyman. *History of the Town of Cornwall, Vermont.* Cornwall, Vt.: Register, 1862.

Matz, Marc, and Heidi Pribell. *The Collections of Cornelia Van Rensselaer Hartman.* Cambridge, Mass.: Marc Matz and Heidi Pribell, 1989.

Memoirs of Members of the Social Circle in Concord, Second Series, From 1795 to 1840. Cambridge, Mass.: Riverside Press, 1888.

Morse, Abner. *Genealogical Register of the Inhabitants of Sherborn and Holliston.* Boston: Damrell and Moor, 1856.

Nantucket, Mass., VR: *Vital Records of Nantucket to the Year 1850.* 5 vols. Boston: NEHGS, 1927.

Nelson, Harold B. "Good Fortune and Good Timing: Collecting American Samplers in Southern California." *Magazine Antiques* 180, no. 3 (May/June 2013): 144–151.

New Bedford, Mass., VR: *Vital Records of New Bedford, Massachusetts, to the Year 1850.* Boston: NEHGS, 1932.

Newbury, Mass., VR: *Vital Records of Newbury, Massachusetts.* 2 vols. Salem, Mass.: Essex Institute, 1911.

Newburyport, Mass., VR: *Vital Records of Newburyport, Massachusetts, to the End of the Year 1849.* 2 vols. Salem, Mass.: Essex Institute, 1911.

Newell, Aimee E. *A Stitch in Time: The Needlework of Aging Women in Antebellum America.* Athens: Ohio University Press, 2014.

New Hampshire, Death and Burial Records Index, 1654–1939. Online database, Ancestry.com, 2011. Also available through the Bureau of Historical Records, Concord, N.H.

New Hampshire, Marriage Records Index, 1637–1947. Online database, Ancestry.com, 2011. Also available through the Bureau of Historical Records, Concord, N.H.

Panno, Natalie. "'Ten thousand times ten thousand worlds': Phebe Folger's Recueil and the Transformation of Quaker Women's Culture in the Early American Republic." A.B. thesis. Harvard University, 2009.

Parker, Theodore. *John Parker of Lexington and His Descendants.* Worcester, Mass.: C. Hamilton, 1893.

Pendle, George. "Size Doesn't Matter at the Met." *The Daily Art, Exhibitions.* 24 February 2016.

Pierce, Frederick C. *The Descendants of John Whitney, who came from London, England to Watertown, Massachusetts, in 1635*. Chicago, Ill.: Conkey Company, 1895.

Pownalborough, Maine, VR: "Pownalborough Marriage Intentions, 1760–1780." Maine Genealogy Archives drawn from *Bangor Historical Magazine*. Vol. 4. Bangor, Maine: J. W. Porter, 1889.

Pringle, James R. *History of the Town and City of Gloucester, Cape Ann, Massachusetts*. Gloucester, Mass.: privately printed, 1892.

Ring, Betty. "Collecting American Samplers Today." In *Needlework: An Historical Survey*. Edited by Betty Ring, 87–93. New York: Universe, 1979.

Rockport, Mass., VR: *Vital Records of Rockport, Massachusetts, to the End of the Year 1749*. Salem, Mass.: Essex Institute, 1924.

Rowley, Mass., VR: *Vital Records of Rowley, Massachusetts, to the End of the Year 1849*. Salem, Mass.: Essex Institute, 1928.

Rumford, Beatrix. *American Folk Portraits from the Abby Aldrich Folk Art Center* . . . . Boston: New York Graphic Society; Williamsburg, Va.: Colonial Williamsburg Foundation, 1981.

Schaffner, Cynthia V. A., and Susan Klein. *Folk Hearts: A Celebration of the Heart Motif in American Folk Art*. New York: Knopf, 1984.

Schoelwer, Susan P., ed. *Lions and Eagles and Bulls: Early American Tavern and Inn Signs from the Connecticut Historical Society*. Hartford: Connecticut Historical Society and Princeton University Press, 2000.

Sebba, Anne M. *Samplers*. New York: Thames and Hudson, 1979.

Sherborn, Mass., VR: *Vital Records of Sherborn, Massachusetts, to the Year 1850*. Boston: NEHGS, 1911.

Sinnett, Charles N. *Richard Pinkham of Old Dover, New Hampshire, and His Descendants*. Concord, N.H.: Rumford Printing, 1908.

Sons of the American Revolution. Application file for Charles Stewart Channell, son of Abram Fitz-John Channell and Welthy Cox, 9 January 1858.

Sotheby's. *The Joan Stephens Collection: Important Samplers and Pictorial Needlework*. Introduction by Betty Ring. New York: Sotheby's, 1997.

Sotheby Parke Bernet, Inc. *Important Frakturs, Embroidered Pictures, Theorem Paintings and Cutwork Pictures and Other American Folk Art: from the Collection of Edgar William and Bernice Chrysler Garbisch, Part III . . . Nov. 12, 1974 . . . Sale number 3692*. New York: Sotheby Parke-Bernet, 1974.

Sprague, Warren Vincent. *Sprague Families in America*. Rutland, Vt.: Tuttle Co., 1913.

Staples, Kathleen. "Embroidered Evidence: Family Record Samplers in the Revolutionary War Pension Files of the National Archives, Washington, D.C." Presented at "Embroidery: The Thread of History," Winterthur Museum, 20 October 2018.

Starbuck, Alexander. *A Century of Free Masonry in Nantucket*. Nantucket, Mass.: NHA, 1903.

Starbuck, Alexander. *The History of Nantucket: County, Island and Town*. Boston: Goodspeed, 1924.

Stearns, Ezra S. *History of Ashburnham, Massachusetts*. Boston: Published by the Town by J. E. Farwell and Co., 1887.

Swan, Marshall W. S. *Town on Sandy Bay: A History of Rockport, Massachusetts*. Canaan, N.H.: Town History Committee, 1980.

Swan, Marshall W. S. to the author, 16 December 1986.

Swan, Susan B. *Plain and Fancy: American Women and Their Needlework, 1700–1850*. New York: Holt, Rinehart, Winston, 1977.

Taylor, Edward. "To the Family Relict." Quoted in *The Puritans in America: A Narrative Anthology*, edited by Alan Heimert, 331. Cambridge: Harvard University Press, 1985.

Tillou, Peter H., and Paul F. Rovetti. *Nineteenth-Century Folk Painting: Our Spirited National Heritage. Works of Art from the Collection of Mr. and Mrs. Peter Tillou*. Storrs, Conn.: William Benton Museum, 1973.

Townsend, Mass., VR: *Vital Records of Townsend, Massachusetts, to the end of the Year 1873*. Boston: NEHGS, 1992.

United States Federal Census, 1830. Online database, Ancestry.com, 2010.

United States Federal Census, 1880. Online database, Ancestry.com and the Church of Jesus Christ of Latter-day Saints, 2018.

United States, Sons of the American Revolution Membership Applications, 1889–1970. Online database, Ancestry.com, 2011.

Van Wagenen, Avis Stearns. *Genealogy and Memoirs of Isaac Stearns and His Descendants.* 2 vols. Syracuse, N.Y.: Courier Printing, 1901.

Waltham, Mass., VR: *Vital Records of Waltham, Massachusetts, to the year 1850.* Boston: NEHGS, 1904.

The Warwick Collection: Cheever Family Record. Notes compiled by Peter and Leslie Warwick, Middletown, N.J. Author's archives.

Watertown, Mass., VR: *Watertown Records comprising the First and Second Books of Town Proceedings. . . .* Watertown, Mass.: Fred C. Barker, 1894.

Watkins, Malcolm C. "Smithsonian Preview." *Magazine Antiques* 85, no. 1 (January 1964): 86–87.

Webster, Noah. *American Spelling Book.* Hartford: Hudson and Goodwin, 1787.

Webster, Noah. *American Spelling Book.* Revised impression. Hartford: Hudson and Goodwin, 1809.

Webster, Noah. "Dissertation 1." In *Dissertations on the English Language . . . .* Boston: for the author by Isaiah Thomas and Co., 1789.

Weston, Mass., VR: *Town of Weston. Births, Deaths and Marriages, 1707–1850.* Boston: McIndoe Bros., Printers, 1901.

Wheeler, Albert Galatin. *The Genealogical and Encyclopedic History of the Wheeler Family in America.* 2 vols. Boston: American College of Genealogy, 1914.

Wheeler, Richard A. *History of the Town of Stonington, Connecticut . . . 1900.* Mystic, Conn.: L. Verry, 1966.

White, Almira Larkin. *Genealogy of the Ancestors and Descendants of John White.* 2 vols. Haverhill, Mass.: Chase Brothers, Printers, 1900.

Whitman, Roscoe O. *History and Genealogy of the Ancestors and Some Descendants of Stukely Westcott.* 2 vols. Oneonta, N.Y.: Otsego Publishing, 1932.

Whitman, Zachariah G. *The History of the Ancient and Honorable Artillery Company of Massachusetts (Revised and Enlarged), From Its Formation in 1637 and Charter in 1638, to the Present Time . . . .* 2d ed. Boston: John H. Eastburn, Printer, 1842.

Woburn, Mass., VR: *Woburn Records of Births, Deaths, and Marriages.* 10 vols. Boston: Winship, Daniels and Co., 1890–1919.

Young, David C. *Early Families of Sabattus, Androscoggin County, Maine: Formerly part of Greene, Lewiston, Lisbon, Bowdoin and West Bowdoinham.* Danville, Maine: privately printed, 1998.

Young, E. Harold. *History of Pittsfield, New Hampshire.* Pittsfield, N.H.: Town, 1953.

Website Sources for Images and Data

Alderfer Auction, 501 Fairgrounds Rd., Hatfield, Pa. 19440.

American Ancestors, NEHGS. www.americanancestors.org/DB503/i/0/1/0.

Antique Associates at West Townsend, Inc., 473 Main St., West Townsend, Mass. 01474.

Antique Dealers' Association of America, P.O. Box 218, Northwood, N.H. 03261.

AntiqueSampler.com. 40 Ferry Rd., Old Saybrook, Conn.

Axtell Antiques, 1 River St., Deposit, N.Y. 13754.

Copake Auctions Inc., 266 East Main St., Copake, N.Y. 12516.

eBay, Inc., San Jose, Calif. www.ebay.com.

Family Tree Samplers, 1759–1894. Online database, AmericanAncestors.org, NEHGS, 2013. (From the collection of Dan and Marty Campanelli.) www.americanancestors.org/DB503/i/0/1/0.

Garth's Auctioneers and Appraisers, 589 W. Nationwide Blvd., Columbus, Ohio 43215.

John McGinnis Auctions, 76 Main St., Amesbury, Mass. 01913.

Kaminski Auctions, 117 Elliott St., Beverly, Mass. 01915.

Kennedy Galleries, Inc., 730 Fifth Ave., New York City, N.Y. 10019.

Liveauctioneers.com. New York, N.Y.

Maine Antique Digest, Waldoboro, Maine.

M. Finkel and Daughter, *Samplings,* 936 Pine St., Philadelphia, Pa. 19107.

Nantucket Historical Association, *Barney Genealogical Record.* Online database, genealogy.nha.org.

National Society of the Colonial Dames of America. nscda.org/historical-activities/samplers.

Northeast Auctions, now Bourgeault-Horan Antiquarian Associates LLC, 93 Pleasant St., Portsmouth, N.H. 03801.

Prices4Antiques Research Services, P.O. Box 2199, Marietta, Ohio 45750.

Skinner, Inc., 63 Park Plaza, Boston, Mass. 02216. www.skinnerinc.com.

Sotheby's, 1334 York Ave., New York, N.Y. 10021.

United States, Revolutionary War Pension and Bounty-Land-Warrant Application File. Department of the Interior, Bureau of Pensions, National Archives and Records Administration. Online database, Ancestry.com, 2010.

William Reese Company, 409 Temple Street, New Haven, Conn. 06511. Williamreesecompany.com.

Photograph Credits

Figure 3: Ashley Bowen painting, about 1780
    Watercolor, 16 ¾ x 11 ¼ inches (42.545 x 28.575 cm)
    Gift of Mr. Alexander O. Vietor, Esq., 1980 M18658
    Courtesy of Peabody Essex Museum
    Photo by Mark Sexton.

Front cover, Figure 5: William Saville (1770-1853)
    Woodbury/Lane Family Tree, Gloucester, 1795
    Watercolor and pen on paper
    Gift of Mrs. William Doelger, 1976
    Collection of the Cape Ann Museum.

Figure 15: © RMN-Grand Palais / Art Resource, NY.

Figures 20a, 20b, and 23: Drawings by Peter Benes.

Figure 27: Courtesy, Winterthur Museum, Busk, 1782, Strafford, VT, Wood, Gift of Aubigne L. Gergen, John A. Gergen, Kenneth J. Gergen, Stephen L. Gergen and David R. Gergen, 1992.87.

Back cover (top), Figures 28, 29, 30, 38, 39, 40, 45, 48, 52, 53, 54, 126, 135, 136: Courtesy of the Nantucket Historical Association Research Library.

Figure 31: colonialnorthamerica.library.harvard.edu/990096146580203941, f. 31v. (seq. 66).

Figure 32: colonialnorthamerica.library.harvard.edu/990096146580203941, f. 53v. (seq. 110).

Figures 43, 102: Images courtesy of Northeast Auctions.

Figures 47, 101: Hannah Kelleher, Courtesy of Pook and Pook, Inc.

Figure 63: William Saville (1770-1853)
    Dennison/Griffin Family Tree, Gloucester 1815
    Watercolor and pen on paper
    Collection of the Cape Ann Museum.

Figure 65: John Parnell, American Folk Art Museum / Art Resource, NY.

Figures 68, 70, 73, 114, 115, 130, 131: Peter Benes.

Figures 71 and 72: Photographs provided by *Kennedy Quarterly*, Kennedy Galleries, Inc., New York.

Back cover (bottom), Figure 77: Courtesy of the Huntington Art Museum, San Marino, California.

Figure 84: Courtesy, Winterthur Museum, Genealogical sampler by Lorenza Fisk, 1811, Massachusetts, Silk, Linen, Gift of Mrs. Alfred C. Harrison, 1969.430.

Figure 89: Courtesy, Winterthur Museum, Family register by S. Morton, 1806-1815, Stephentown, NY, Ink, Watercolor, Laid paper, Prussian blue, Iron brown, Museum purchase, 1960.324.

Figures 90, 113: Samuel Pennington, *Maine Antique Digest*, April 1979 and September 1987.

Figure 96: Carl Voellings, Antique Associates of West Townsend, Inc.

Figure 99: Barb Mardis, Courtesy of Susan Jaquith and descendants of George Dinsmore and Mary Sivona Davis Jaquith.

Figure 111: J. David Bohl.

Figure 120: Robert and Elizabeth McKay, Redbank, N.J.

Figures 122, 138: Gregory H. Laing.

Figure 123: Photograph courtesy of Pam Boynton.

Figure 132: Photograph courtesy of Marc Matz and Heidi Pribell.

Endpapers: Map reproductions courtesy of the Norman B. Leventhal Map & Education Center at the Boston Public Library.

Name Index

This index contains the principal names of children and parents specified in the checklist, the text, and the captions, but not those that only appear as names in the family registers. Numbers in bold font refer to pages with images.

General Index

This index contains all other names, topics, symbol types, locations, professions, and appropriate sources. Numbers in bold font refer to pages with images.